Essays in Economics
Theories, Facts, and Policies

VOLUME TWO

Essays in Economics
Theories, Facts, and Policies

VOLUME TWO

Wassily Leontief

M. E. SHARPE, INC./WHITE PLAINS, NEW YORK

Library of Congress Catalog Card Number: 77-79062
International Standard Book Number: 0-87332-092-1

Printed in the United States of America.

The author gratefully acknowledges permission to reprint from the following publishers:
Indiana University Press for translation of Essay I in *Foundations of Soviet Strategy for
Economic Growth—Selected Short Soviet Essays 1924–1930*, edited by N. Spulber, copyright
© 1964 by Indiana University Press; *The American Economic Review* for Essays III and VIII; *The
Review of Economics and Statistics* for Essays IV and VI; North-Holland Publishing Company
for Essays V and IX; and New York University Press for Essay XI, originally published in the
Charles C. Moskowitz Memorial Lectures of the College of Business and Public Administration
at New York University, *The Economic System in an Age of Discontinuity: Long-Range
Planning or Market Reliance?* by Wassily Leontief and Herbert Stein, copyright © 1976 by New
York University.

To Estelle

Foreword

This second volume of my essays comes out ten years after the first, which was published in 1966 and has recently been reprinted as Volume I of the present edition. Most of the pieces included in Volume II appeared in various symposia and periodicals after 1967, but some came out before.

The sequence of chapters is thematic rather than strictly chronological, and some take up and develop further themes already sounded in Volume I.

Essays I and II were originally published half a century ago. The first treats the question of national accounts, while the second examines the measurement of industrial concentration with the aim of identifying the theoretical rationale of what, at that time, was approached as a question of simple statistical description.

"Theoretical Assumptions and Nonobserved Facts" is the presidential address read before the annual meeting of the American Economic Association in 1970. The criticism of the speculative orientation of contemporary economic theory, particularly in its mathematical version, had been noted before in the Foreword to the first volume.

In "An Alternative to Aggregation in Input-Output Analysis and National Accounts" and "The Dynamic Inverse," the solution of two classical theoretical problems is approached in structural input-output terms. In "Environmental Repercussions and the Economic Structure: An Input-Output Approach" and "National Income, Economic Structure, and Environmental Externalities," the same method is employed to develop an operational approach to environmental problems.

Two papers—"An International Comparison of Factor Costs and Factor Use: A Review Article" and "Explanatory Power of the Comparative Cost Theory of International Trade and Its Limits"—address the problems of international trade. The "Structure of the World Economy" is the Nobel lecture, in which I present a proposal for the application of the input-output method to the detailed factual explanation of the international division of labor and a systematic general equilibrium analysis of the structure of interregional trade. Even while this Foreword is being written, a large multiregional, multisectoral model of the world economy has already been constructed and is about to be published under the auspices of the United Nations.

The last essay, entitled "National Economic Planning: Methods and Problems," contains a further development of the ideas and proposals originally advanced in a paper included as the last chapter of Volume I.

WASSILY LEONTIEF

West Burke, Vermont

Contents

Essays in Economics
Theories, Facts, and Policies

VOLUME TWO

I

The balance of the economy of the USSR

A METHODOLOGICAL ANALYSIS OF THE WORK OF
THE CENTRAL STATISTICAL ADMINISTRATION

Among various problems which must be solved by contemporary Russian statistics, that of representing in numbers the total turnover of economic life is perhaps the most interesting as well as the most complex. As a result of many years' work by the Central Statistical Administration, the "Balance of the Economy of the USSR in 1923/24" has appeared.[1] The principal feature of this balance, in comparison with such economic-statistical investigations as the American and the English censuses, is the attempt to represent in numbers not only the production but also the distribution of the social product, so as to obtain a general picture of the entire process of reproduction in the form of a *tableau économique* (economic table).

On the income side of the balance is presented the value of the total amount of goods at the disposal of the whole economy during the year under consideration.

All these goods are divided three ways into separate groups. First, the three large-scale branches of the economy—industry, agriculture, and construction—are separated from one another. Second, all the goods created are divided into four groups in accordance with, so to speak, their functional relationships to the process of production: (1) goods intended for individual consumption (production factor:

Originally published in Russian under the title "Balans narodnogo khoziaistva SSSR" in *Planovoe khoziaistvo*, No. 12, 1925. English translation from N. Spulber (ed.), *Foundations of Soviet Strategy for Economic Growth—Selected Short Soviet Essays 1924–1930* (Bloomington: Indiana University Press, 1964), pp. 88–94.
[1] *Ekonomicheskaia zhizn'*, No. 72 of the current year [1925]. Report by P. I. Popov in the Council for Labor and Defense (STO).

labor); (2) raw and other materials; (3) fuels; and (4) tools of production. Finally, all values are broken down, in accordance with the formation of prices, into their component parts, which jointly add up to consumer prices—namely, local production prices, transportation expenditures, and trade markups.

On the expenditure side, the table shows how the values representing the national economy's income are distributed and used. The distribution of expenditures follows in general the subdivisions of income. The values are divided, according to their origin, into three main groups: products of industry, products of agriculture, and products of construction. The relationship to the process of production is again denoted by subdivisions into (1) consumer goods; (2) raw and other materials; (3) fuels; and (4) tools of production. All goods, whether used in production (namely, in its three main branches), in the process of distribution (transport and trade), or in consumption, are divided into three main groups according to their economic rather than their production and technical functions. They thus find their expression in the income data, which distinguish among expenditures for production, transportation, and trade.

Clearly, this balance scheme is based on the methodological principle of exclusively material accounting. Only material goods are accounted for. The income side of the economic turnover is considered only insofar as it consists of "objectivized" material goods. From this point of view it is fully consistent that the public administration, whose budget has reached almost 1.5 billion rubles, should be represented in the balance by only 475.7 million rubles. The state does not create any material goods; its income is "derived" and as such does not have any counterpart in the income of the economic balance. But neither do its expenditures, for example, the payments without material counterpart to second parties such as officials; these are also treated as "secondary" (derived) income. Inasmuch as state establishments act as immediate consumers, the corresponding expenditures are reflected in the category of collective consumption. The same device is applied to transportation. Its services are taken into consideration only to the extent that they enter as costs in the prices of goods; consequently, passenger traffic has been omitted.

Although this methodological peculiarity limits the attempt to make the balance represent a complete picture of the turnover of the economy, it nevertheless leaves the internal organic structure of the balance scheme untouched. The same thing cannot be said with regard to the concept and the method of calculation of the total income of the economy. This problem has great importance for the methodology of the entire statistics of production, and in the case of generalizations about the balance, its role becomes decisive. For example, in the accounting of "value added"—whose purpose is to calculate the net income of the economy—if total product constitutes only an intermediate item, then the "dualistic" concept of the total product represents the model as well as the basic element of the entire balance system.

Let us, therefore, briefly touch upon the general formulation of this problem, since only in this way can we critically evaluate the method which has been used in this scheme.

The total product is the result of the process of production, which, in addition to newly created values, also contains the value of the goods expended and worn out in its creation.

This latter value is usually called costs. In statistical methodology, the definite distinction between these two value sums means that the first of these sums—the net product—can appear no more than once in the process of production. Cost expenditures, on the contrary, can endlessly pass from one stage of production to another and reappear at each stage in the same form. Thus the net product of several branches of production is always equal to the sum of the individual net products; costs, on the contrary, amount to less than the sum of the individual total products, since they constitute only a part of the total value of production and since the same values are accounted again and again in various technically related processes of production. This reasoning, which appears somewhat complicated in abstract form, will become clearer in a numerical example. Let us imagine a complex branch of industry with three production stages. On the first—the lowest stage—a value (net product) of one unit is added to the value of expended raw materials and other expenditures equaling 2 units.

In this way, total product consists in $2 + 1 = 3$. Further processing occurs at the second stage. To the 3 units, which occur here as expenditures, 4 new ones are added. Consequently, total product comprises $3 + 4 = 7$. In its turn, the second production stage is included in the third and last stage, where to these 7 units 5 more

Table 1—Growth of value in the total product

STAGES	COSTS	NET PRODUCT	TOTAL PRODUCT
I	2	+ 1	= 3
II	3	+ 4	= 7
III	7	+ 5	= 12
Total	12	+ 10	= 22

are added. The values of costs, of the net product, and of the total product of all three stages are summed up in Table 1.

But if we imagine the same process of production as a single phenomenon, then the corresponding formula will appear as 2 + 10 = 12, where the first figure represents costs; the second, the net product; and their total, the total product. A comparison with the first conclusion shows that the sum of the net product remains the same in both cases (10); the costs, on the contrary, which were expressed by 12 value units in the first method, are expressed by 2 units in the second method thanks to the exclusion of all double counting. In accordance with this, the sum of the total product amounts to 22 units in the first case and 12 in the second. Each of these two magnitudes of the total product—the real one, i.e., that found after excluding any double counting (equal to 12 in our example), as well as the second, designated by us as the "total turnover" (equal to 22 in our example)—has a scientific meaning. The total turnover is more suitable for balance accounting than the real sum, for the same reason that the real gross product is much more suitable than the net product: the more deeply and widely individual relationships are included, the more clearly the organic structure of the economic whole appears. On the other hand, however, it is much more difficult to obtain a total turnover which can be applied in a scientific way than to obtain a corresponding real magnitude.

Every statistical sum should be constituted in such a way that the relationship among the values of its component parts fully corresponds to the actual relationships of individual data included in the subject of statistical investigation. Both component parts of the real sum of the gross product—the net product as well as the original costs, i.e., those computed without any double counting—are accurate and indisputable. For this reason the requirement mentioned above is automatically fulfilled to a certain degree.

The matter of the total turnover is completely different. We have seen above that double calculation consists in considering the same value of costs repeatedly in several parts of a connected process of production. The larger the number of these partial stages, the greater the extent of such double counting, and the greater the corresponding total turnover. If the total turnovers of several branches of industry are to be compared with one another, the dissection of all these processes of production, which is necessary for such a calculation, should be performed in a uniform manner. Such dissection can be undertaken from two points of view. The first is the technical point of view. In this case the various stages of production which are technically analogous are looked upon as separate subjects of calculation. If, for instance, the individual branches of production of the textile industry are to be compared with one another, the production of yarn and fabrics of each branch—cotton, silk, and wool—should be computed and totaled. We thus obtain several total turnovers, computed in an identical manner, whose comparison is methodologically possible; but such a method can lead us to our goal only in the case where a statistical investigation is limited to a narrow circle of related areas of production.

If branches of industry which do not have anything in common technically are included in the investigation, this method will be completely inapplicable; there can be, for instance, no question of analogous stages of production in machine construction and paper production. In an economic balance, however, not just some but all the areas of the economy are compared, and the above method is, as a result, inapplicable. But even in this case various objects of investigation can be reduced to a common denominator, if the necessary dissection is performed from an *economic* point of view. The calculation is based not on any technically separate stages of production, but on economic unity. The total turnover will be the sum of the values of goods which are sold on the free market by the individual enterprises active in the given process of production. It is thus equal to the sum of goods produced by the corresponding enterprises.

Such a method provides a possibility of comparing the economic weight of all the areas of production with one another, leaving aside their technical peculiarities. But even this method is not always applicable; its limitations are greater than those of the method mentioned earlier. Economic dissection of the process of production is possible only when the latter is organized as in a barter economy, while the total amount of goods can be computed only with reference to a commodity economy. Like the ideal socialist economy, a large number of isolated natural economies do not know any intermediate economic division of labor and, consequently, any double economic calculation of costs. Since, for a balanced statistical comparison, subdivisions performed from a technical point of view are insufficient, it follows that the total turnover should be renounced and the real gross product be considered instead. But if the economy is organized partly as a barter economy and partly as a natural economy, a coherent picture of the whole can be obtained only through the computation of the real total income, since this is applicable to all economic systems, whereas the method of the total turnover—as we have seen—is not applicable to the branches of production with a natural economy (at least not to the extent necessary for balanced accounting). The following circumstance must also be taken into consideration: inasmuch as individual branches of production interpenetrate one another to a greater or lesser extent by means of exchange, a certain double counting will take place in totaling their real gross product. Thus the total national gross product will constitute the sum of the turnovers. But a methodological danger will appear only in the case where a comparison with another total national gross product is undertaken.

Let us now turn to the main published table of the balance of production and distribution. The size of the shares marketed by each branch shows that the economy of our Union is still organized, in the main, as a natural economy. Agriculture sells a comparatively small part of its products; the largest part is used by the farm households. Nevertheless, the method of total turnover was applied here. Furthermore, the subdivision of agricultural production shows that the calculation of the total turnover was based on technical dissection: cultivation of the soil and of meadows, animal husbandry, forestry, fishing, and hunting. This method should be recognized as wholly wrong. As we have seen, such a method inevitably leads to a series of discrepancies, since there is no principle on the basis of which an objective calculation can be made of the total amounts of the total product of individual branches of production. Hence it is completely meaningless to compare the shares of the total products obtained in the various branches of production "per worker engaged in production" or "per capita" of the population (as shown in the balance table).

The balance does not give any references to the sources which served as foundations of its construction. Four categories of data can be assumed: (1) current statistics; (2) censuses, namely, the general population and industrial census of 1920 and the urban census of 1923; (3) statistics of the budget; and (4) other sources as, for instance, the data of state and trade organizations, of the cooperatives, etc.

As the first attempt of our statistics, the balance needs further methodological discussion. And such discussion will acquire a firm foundation only with the publication of all materials and with the indication of the methods used for their processing.

II

The theory and statistical description of concentration

I

Any purposeful statistical investigation of a phenomenon requires a special conceptual apparatus, a theory, that will enable the investigator to select from among the numberless multitude of facts those that prospectively fit into some pattern and hence are susceptible to systematization. Even such a relatively simple event as a shift in population must first be placed within a rather complicated conceptual framework before it can be dealt with directly in a statistical investigation. The more complicated the object of inquiry, the more important its theoretical "preparation," so to speak. Accordingly, we too are obliged to erect the requisite theoretical framework before we proceed to the purely statistical aspect of our topic.

Production and industry are comprised of a number of particular processes taking place both in parallel to one another and at different levels. Economic development entails not only the accession of new units and the elimination of many old ones, but also a continuous process of structural change in what is retained; there are two basic aspects to such change that evolve side by side: differentiation and integration.[1]

This qualitative change is accompanied by another, quantitative change: the size of the individual economic units (cells) changes, just

Originally published in German under the title "Über die Theorie und Statistik der Konzentration," in *Jahrbücher für Nationalökonomie und Statistik*, Vol. 126, March 1927. Translation by Michel Vale.
[1] Schulze-Gävernitz, *Der Grossbetrieb* (Leipzig, 1892), p. 88.

as do the overall proportions of the economic system as a whole. These two processes are quite different and totally independent of each other; this is clear from the fact that they can proceed in different directions at the same time. Let us look more closely at the latter of these two processes.

The question may be formulated as follows: What are the effective factors that give rise to quantitative changes in individual production units? (We shall forego a more precise definition of these terms for the time being.)

II

Every production process brings together into a unified, coordinated whole various factors of production. By this we mean simply all types of outlays, such as, for example, those that are enumerated as individual items in the most detailed accounting ledger of an industrial enterprise; by productive factors we do not mean, then, any basic unit or primary factor that cannot be broken down further.

Individual productive factors come together in definite proportions, not in any random quantities. For example, a woodcutter works with one axe. Two workers, however, are needed to use a two-handed saw; three would already be too many, and one not enough—that is, in the first case the workers, and in the second the saw, would not be adequately utilized. Without adducing further examples, we may formulate the following proposition: for every production process there exist some ideal proportions in which all the factors of production involved in that process must be brought together.

Cassel calls this relationship the "technical coefficient."[2] It should be borne in mind, however, that the choice among different factors of production serving the same end depends on their prices; hence, to speak of a specific technical coefficient has meaning only if a specific price level is assumed beforehand.

There is yet another consideration of decisive importance for our discussion: individual factors of production can be used only in quite specific quantities, not in just any arbitrary ones. With the right number of workers, one, two, three, and more saws may be used,

[2] *Theoretische Sozialökonomie* (Leipzig, 1921), p. 119.

but never ½, 1½, or 2½ saws. There exists some basic, indivisible quantum.

Thus, a production process will have attained its optimal form only if it is large enough in scope so that the proportions in which the factors of production are present permit the fullest utilization of all basic units. Of course, in this case the crucial factors are those for which the smallest number of indivisible basic units is required in order for them to participate in the production process. For example, if three types of productive factors—such as power-generating equipment, machinery for the actual fabrication, and labor—are involved in the production of an item in the proportions 1:10:200, a factory must employ at least 1 power unit (such as an electric motor), 10 productive machines, and 200 men. If, then, a technological invention made it possible to manufacture electric motors that were half as big as those in our initial example, yet performed just as efficiently, the optimal proportions, and hence peak performance, could be achieved with a (small) power motor and only 5 fabricating machines and 100 men (the proportions in this case would be 1:5:100). On the other hand, the introduction of fabricating machines that were half as big would have no relevance with regard to determining the minimal size of our factory, since the "power-source" factor is an indivisible unit, while the amounts of the other factors could not be reduced without destroying the proportionality. The indicated minimum limit is also a maximum limit, that is, it is an optimum point; no special demonstration of this should be necessary. After the minimum size has been reached, production can be expanded efficiently only by constructing new production units of the same kind, not by expanding the old, if the correct proportionality is to be maintained. Any attempt to expand on existing plant would cause a shift in the proportionality.[3] There is no need to demonstrate at length that all the propositions we have explained on the basis of our "technical" example are equally valid with regard to organizational expenses and other "management costs."[4]

[3] We shall not make the usual distinction between constant and variable costs (e.g., K. Bücher, "Das Gesetz der Massenproduktion," in *Entstehung der Volkswirtschaft*, collection II [Tübingen, 1918]) in our discussion, since such a distinction is not at all absolute, only relative. See J. M. Clark, *Economics of Overhead Costs* (1923).
[4] "The costs of intellectual equipment, then, are one of the big sources of economy in large scale production" (Clark, op. cit., p. 120).

It should be borne in mind, however, that the two magnitudes necessary for determining optimal size—that is, the efficient proportions among the individual factors of production and the size of their elementary units—are by no means constant; they are variables, and any change in them brings about a corresponding change in the optimal size of the particular production unit.

Therein lies the answer to our question. The quantitative change in the size at individual production and trading units is caused by the tendency toward optimization. If the optimum lies beyond the actual size, the tendency will be toward "concentration"; if it is below the actual size, there will be a tendency toward "decentralization."[5] The former is dominant today, but it is just this current state of things that we wish to explore statistically; here we are dealing with what is possible, not with what is.

For the time being, we should like to avoid, if we may, a time-consuming discussion of the wide array of definitions of the concept of "concentration"; most are merely descriptive and do not differ in substance from ours.[6] We should like only to call attention to a few outwardly very similar but in reality fundamentally different phenomena that often are not distinguished clearly enough from those we have just analyzed.

First, the tendency to conglomerate into monopolies. At issue here is not the absolute size of an individual industrial unit, but its size relative to the magnitude of the particular branch of production. This overall magnitude, however, exhibits completely different patterns of development from those seen in the internal tendency toward concentration.

[5] "The most recent development [of the English textile industry] shows an increase in the number of factories and a decrease in the number of workers. From 1890 to 1903 the number of cotton mills in Great Britain increased from 2,363 to 2,476, while according to the census figures the number of workers decreased from 565,000 in 1891 to 546,000 in 1901" (G. Brodnitz, "Betriebskonzentration und Kleinbetrieb in der englischen Industrie," *Jahrbücher für Nationalökonomie und Statistik*, Series III, Vol. 35(1908), 188).

[6] Lexical definition: "The most usual distinction between a large concern and a small concern is based on the amount of capital invested in an enterprise (!)" (*Handwörterbuch d. Staatswiss.*," 3rd ed., Vol. V, p. 67). Further on, the advantages of the large concern are enumerated (just as at one time the advantages of the division of labor were listed): (1) division of labor; (2) more favorable market conditions; (3) better cost structure; (4) cheaper credit. Actually these "advantages" can all be brought under point 3.

Second, there is "locational" concentration. This phenomenon also differs fundamentally from real centralization because it represents a purely mechanical agglomeration in the number of independent industrial units—independent, in any case, from the standpoint of the production process.

Of course, one could object that the statistician is interested in the phenomena themselves, not their causes, and hence is quite right to lump together phenomena that are outwardly similar yet may be quite different in their essential properties. This objection would indeed be valid if a statistical description could limit itself to a mere counting operation. Its tasks, however, are much deeper than that: like abstract theoretical science, it too looks for regularities. The methods are different, but the goal is always the same. It would therefore be quite inappropriate to neglect the findings of theoretical analysis in making a statistical investigation.

III

The definition of this tendency toward concentration (unfortunately we do not have a single term that would include both concentration and decentralization) delimits the domain of inquiry of concentration statistics. The next problem we shall take up is that of the measuring unit to be used. We shall approach this problem by means of theoretical analysis as well.

So far, we have regarded the production process as if the individual forces of production were inseparably linked, and hence all had to participate together in the production process. Graphically, this interaction might be described by a number of arrows pointing toward a single point; the final product would be an arrow emerging from the other side of the point (Fig. 1). However, a complex production process may often be broken down into a large number of stages: the various productive factors do not all act together simultaneously; first one and then another is operative.

This is a vertical breakdown; a horizontal breakdown is also possible since the elementary units of many productive factors allow some breakdown of their functions although they themselves are not divisible. For example, half of a generator cannot be used, but its function, in the form of the electric current it produces, can be divided up into

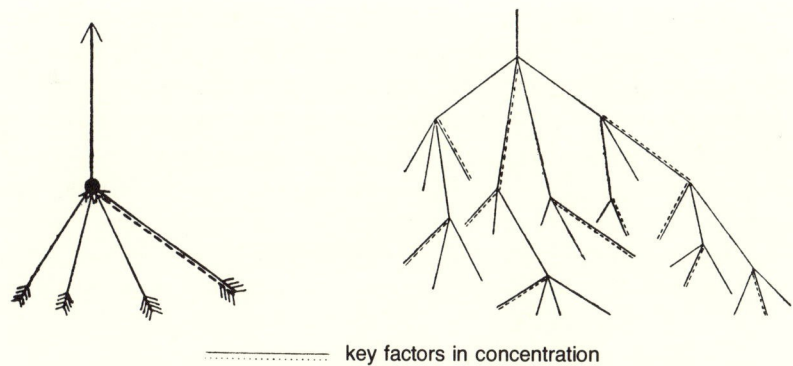

.... key factors in concentration

Figure 1 Figure 2

any number of small portions. Thus, the complex and indivisible marketing organization of a modern large enterprise, or a retail sales chain, can be used by many discrete, independent production units. This fact is of central importance in determining the optimal size of production units. The correct—that is, the most efficient— proportions for the individual factors of production often cannot be brought into line with one another directly. For example, let us suppose that in the above example there is another, fourth factor in addition to the "power unit" factor, the 10 fabrication machines, and the 200 workers, namely a factory building, and that for technical efficiency the entire production process has to be carried out in two large areas. Now, however, let us suppose that the power unit can only be used when everything is located in one area. The coefficient of proportionality of the building factor would thus be 2 and would stand in a 1:1 ratio to the "power unit" productive factor. There are three possibilities: build a larger, that is, less efficient, work space; install two power sources of appropriate design in two separate buildings (in that case, however, only half of their capacity would be used); or, finally, use two smaller power sources of less efficient design. The final choice of one of these three compromises will depend on the prices of the competing individual factors of production; but whichever is ultimately chosen, some reduction in efficiency will be the price that must be paid.

If, on the other hand, an electric power source of the same capacity is used, the other three factors of production could be arranged into two secondary, subsidiary optimal subgroups organized on the basis of the elementary unit of the productive factor "buildings."

Interpreted from this point of view, modern economic organization represents a composite system of concentration units, each wholly contained in the next larger unit and varying in size from a small workshop to an international commercial enterprise. The relationships existing among them may be represented graphically as a multibranched system of groups of arrows (Fig. 2).

IV

Each of these concentration units may be regarded as a census unit or counting unit for statistical purposes. This does not mean, however, that all units may be lumped together. Any statistical study requires that every system be composed of equivalent units. In our case, the type of unit is determined by the extent of the concentration possibilities, which in turn are dependent on the nature of the productive factors involved, the size of their elementary units, and their coefficients of proportionality.

In regard to the first criterion, there is almost no limit as to what productive factors may be considered as being of the same kind; one need only expand the category to include more items (for example, drills, machine tools, productive machines, machinery in general, technical aids, in ascending order). But much of what might be gained by this method would be lost when the other two elements—size of basic units and coefficients of proportionality—are brought into the picture.

Strictly speaking, the technical coefficient is an invariable quantity; that is, even given the entire range of specificity and diversity of the raw materials, special machines, and so on, used in any particular manufacturing process, there really is still only one efficient proportion that exists for them. In this case, the size of the elementary units is also specifically fixed in just the same way. However, as more and more different productive factors are lumped together into one broader, all-embracing category, the particular case loses its specificity, the corresponding coefficient of proportionality becomes less precise, and the resultant statistical aggregate becomes less homogeneous.

It may also happen that concentration units which in reality are of different kinds and different rank—with one actually a constituent part of the other—may be subsumed under the same general term and regarded as equivalent, and thus may be counted as two separate units for census purposes. It would be wrong, however, to try to eliminate this double counting by excluding one of the two. A partial correction here is more dangerous than a systematic error.

V

Now that we have presented the most basic guidelines in at least rough form, let us attempt to assess the actual procedure followed in 1926 in compiling German industrial statistics in the industrial questionnaire and its various appendices. We are quite aware that a criticism of this nature will be quite one-sided, and that the diversity of the tasks involved in a major industrial census—quite apart from the practical difficulties it entails—can be coped with effectively only through a compromise procedure. It is all the more important on that account, however, to be sure that the data obtained in each particular case are usable.

The first problem is the difference between technical and economic units. The technological bias of German industrial statistics has come under sharp criticism for quite some time, but especially since the publication of the final 1907 census report, and the call has been made for a move toward a more economically oriented procedure.[7] This demand was finally met. The results of the 1925 census of industry and trade are classified in terms of "economic units" into eight tables arranged under the letter C.

Normally the particular advantage of these economic units is seen to lie in the fact that, in contrast to specific technical units, they bring together all branches of industry under one common denominator, and hence are especially suited for describing general economic trends. This is not true with regard to the tendency toward concentration, however, as will be clear from a brief reflection on that matter.

---

[7] Conrad, "Die Zählungseinheit der gewerblichen Betriebsstatistik," *Allg. Stat. Arch.*, Vol. 12 (1920); Passow, "Kritische Bemerkungen über den Aufbau unserer gewerblichen Statistik," *Zeitschr. f. Sozialwiss.*, 1911 (also published as an appendix in *Betrieb, Unternehmung, Konzern* [Jena, 1925]).

In question 12 of the industrial questionnaire, independent businesses are all regarded as being of the same type economically. The question now arises: What special place does this type of unit have in the broad hierarchy of concentration units? As we have shown in detail, this position is determined by the special nature of the production and cost factors that come together under this point, of which one plays a decisive role.

To determine this specific cost factor for the economic unit, let us compare two production processes differing only in the fact that one is operated as an independent business while the other is part of a larger economic unit (subsidiary firm). All costs of raw materials, depreciation, internal organization, and administration will be the same; sales and purchasing costs, that is, commercial expenses—the first and last items on the accounting ledger of any independent enterprise—will not exist for the second (subsidiary firm), however. But this is precisely the cost (or productive factor) that might determine the optimal size of the concentrated unit enterprise.

It is quite incomprehensible why such decisive importance should be ascribed to this relatively negligible factor. True, it is encountered in all branches of industry, but this does not mean that it is a decisive concentration factor in every case. The productive factor "power source" is also encountered in almost all branches of industry, yet it would be quite erroneous to say that it has the same significance in a chemical factory as in a machine-building factory.

In quite a large number of cases, technological concentration takes place over the head, as it were, of any breakdown in economic terms. Indeed, this is precisely what makes the social division of labor so unique.[8] On the other hand, in all the analogous cases of conflict analyzed in the foregoing, it is the entrepreneurial—that is, the commercial cost—factor that is sacrificed because of its relatively

[8] An interesting example of this kind of concentration is provided by tenement factories in the English metal products industry: "The tenement factory is a factory building in which accommodations with motor power or even fully equipped small factories, i.e., premises with the requisite machinery and power sources, are hired out to small entrepreneurs" (Brodnitz, op. cit., pp. 188–189).

In German industrial statistics such a factory, with its 300 to 400 "independent" workers, would be broken down into just as many "economic" units and ranked together with the other "independent businesses."

minor importance. Most of the common interest groups, mergers, and trusts typical of today's economic development have come into existence because of a striving for a technological, not an economic, optimum. Of course, economic consolidation is a factor, but it would be just as wrong to consider this economic factor as decisive with regard to concentration as it would be to consider one cause of concentration in the aforementioned example to be the fact that the entire production process was brought under one roof—in itself an inexpedient measure—to accommodate the use of an efficient power source.

We do not wish to deny the possibility that an enterprise, while serving as an economic unit, in many cases can also really represent a concentration unit; but we believe we may validly maintain that, from a purely theoretical viewpoint, no particular arguments can be adduced that would warrant preferring this unit over "technological" units as more advantageous to use as a basic concentration unit for census statistics. In particular, it is wrong to think that it represents any universal standard with which the concentration tendencies present in diverse branches of industry could be reduced to one common denominator.[9]

The technological (i.e., not economic) census units of the industrial census are the following:

1. Local units—local establishments
   a. Independent enterprises
   b. Head offices of independent enterprises
   c. Branch offices geographically separated from the main office
2. Technological (industrial) units in the strict sense; subsidiary factories

As is evident from the definition, all these categories are related in some manner to the enterprise unit—specifically, in such a way that these technological units appear as subordinate to the economic

[9] We should expressly stress that these assertions do not imply a disregard or outright dismissal of the methodological rule that the technological factor must be rigorously kept distinct from the economic factor. In our view, the concentration problem, on the whole, is basically a technological problem. Therefore, the significance ascribed to economic units in the present case is quite different from their role in statistics on national income (see our "Methodologische Untersuchung: Die Bilanz der Russichen Volkswirtschaft," *Weltw. Arch.*, Vol. XXII).

units, as if the latter were the cornerstones of the entire edifice.[10] We have already shown how mistaken it is to approach the matter in this way, since it simply overlooks the bulk of today's trend toward concentration. Indeed, in only two questions of the industrial questionnaire is there anything that could be regarded as even an attempt to pinpoint supraeconomic or intereconomic concentration factors. In question 4 "a cottage worker or tradesman" is asked to give "the name and domicile of the employer—manufacturer, publisher, salesman, etc."—for whom he works. Question 9V asks whether the business (1C) gets its electricity from other sources (electric power plant, long-distance power station, etc.) and (2B) whether electricity is supplied "to other firms or other consumers."

VI

The third and last question, whose answer is just as important for concentration statistics as the first two, is the question of what yardstick should be used to measure the magnitude of various census units.

Although we realize that a "practical" solution to this problem can be obtained only from considerations of a "practical" nature, let us nevertheless pursue our theoretical line of reasoning a little further as we discuss the theoretical foundations of concentration statistics.

There exist two ideal concentration units (ideal in the sense that they satisfy all theoretical principles). The question to be asked is: Assuming an exhaustive knowledge of all productive factors involved and of the production outputs, in what terms may their magnitudes actually be compared?

If all productive factors and technological coefficients of the two units to be compared were equal, then the relative sizes of the two units could be deduced directly from a comparison of any randomly selected individual combination of factors of production. However, we know that the indicated assumptions are valid only for units of the same size; any difference in size is linked directly as a causal factor with differences among either the technical coefficients or the pro-

[10] "The economic unit is the most inclusive of all these statistical units," *Volks-, Berufs- und Betriebszählung*, 1925, instructions for filling out the industrial questionnaire, *Statistisches Reichsamt*, August 1925, p. 1.

ductive factors used. If two production units are of different sizes, then either the factors determining concentration in the two units stand in different proportions to the other productive factors involved, or the latter differ in their degree of efficiency. Any attempt to deduce the overall ratio from a comparison of these concentration-determining factors is doomed to failure in the first case. For instance, to take an extreme example, two factories of different sizes, undergoing concentration with respect to the power source factor, both have a steam power plant. One plant is fully utilized, but the other operates at only half-capacity because of an insufficient number of machines and workers. If the two establishments were compared in terms of the number of power sources, both would be considered the same size, which of course would be quite wrong. It would be more correct, if less exact, to make the comparison in terms of the variable factors, for example, the number of machines or the number of workers; the size of the second factory would have been underestimated in our example, however, to the extent that the unused portion, so to speak, of the power unit was left out of account. When the factors determining concentration are given relatively too little weight, on the other hand, use of this comparative method would give an overestimation.[11]

The material output of a production process is related to this magnitude in the same way as the other "variable" productive factors: as the optimal dimension is approached, the proportion shifts in favor of the output volume. That is of course the entire rationale behind the concentration tendency.

This, however, exhausts the series of possible natural criteria. Thus it proves impossible to make an absolutely accurate comparison of two concentration units by any natural standard.

This leaves only the standard of value. With it, all productive factors can be brought directly together and correctly compared. The other advantage of the standard of value, an advantage associated with

---

[11] Current industrial taxation practices are quite instructive for the industrial statistician. For example, a deliberate bias is given to the technical coefficient measuring the size of an enterprise on the basis of the number of just those productive factors whose share in the production process exceeds the efficient proportion. For example, the size of sugar factories was measured on the basis of the total space occupied by the diffusion equipment in which the sugar sap is extracted from the beets. This led to a more efficient use of space in processing the intermediate products.

its universality, is that it permits a comparison of qualitatively different concentration units.

In practice, industrial units are compared by the following methods:

I. Material standards
    A. Technical equipment
        1. Special equipment—for example, number of spindles in a textile mill
        2. Power capacity of power units
    B. Quantity of products in kind
    C. Number of persons employed
II. Price measures
    A. Value of total productive factors—capital (scarce)
    B. Value of production (American census)[12]

The number of workers is, of course, a generally accepted standard. Its theoretical advantage lies in the fact that, first, it alone of all the "material" standards is universal and, second, the productive factor "labor" can be broken down into relatively small elementary units (in subsidiary factories, even a *part* of human labor power is used) and hence can almost always be regarded as a variable factor of production. It determines concentration only in small businesses and thus should be used as a measure of size only with great caution.[13] Like any indirect method of calculation, comparison with regard to number of workers involves a source of considerable error. Experience has shown that the technical coefficient of the productive factor "labor"

---

[12] Astonishingly, Passow ("Der Anteil der grossen industriellen Unternehmungen am gewerblichen Leben der Gegenwart," *Zeitschr. f. Sozialwiss,*" 1915, p. 491) omits the gross output in his enumeration of the parameters that might be used to measure the "share of large enterprises in industrial life." He considers "net worth" to be the best parameter. "Net proceeds" is not even considered as a measure of concentration, since it is much more difficult to ascertain than gross output, and moreover gives a much less clear picture of the real dimensions. The ratio of net worth to gross worth may be considered an index of the degree of dependence of a concentration unit on the other (higher) concentration units and hence is quite important for an analysis of vertical concentration.

[13] A typical comment is appended to Table 11 (use of motors, broken down by size category, in factories) of Vol. 113 of the *Statistik der Deutschen Reiches*: "The following table covers only principal factories, because for subsidiary factories the personnel and, hence, size categories are disregarded" (p. 396).

has been on a steady decline, while industrial concentration units have been moving upward toward an optimal size. Thus, in 1895 in Germany there were an average of 5.1 employed workers per horse-power of the power units in all factories employing 1 to 5 persons; for factories employing 6 to 20 persons, 31 to 100 persons, and 101 to 1,000 persons, this figure was 3.2, 2.3, and 1.3, respectively, and so on.[14] The true proportion is thus shifted in favor of the smaller units by the remaining classification.

[14] Calculated according to figures given in Table 15 of Vol. 113 of the *Statistik der Deutschen Reiches* (pp. 528–529). The relationship between labor force and output for different size categories is illustrated by the following example from the milling industry:

ANNUAL PRODUCTION OF MILL (IN 100 KG UNITS)	100 KG PER WORKING DAY
up to 3,000	8.77
3,001–6,000	10.57
6,001–12,000	11.55
12,001–18,000	11.50
18,001–30,000	10.45
30,001–60,000	11.28
60,001–90,000	11.06
90,001–120,000	12.48
120,001–150,000	15.68
150,001–180,000	13.27
180,001–240,000	13.10
240,001–300,000	15.92
300,001–450,000	16.78
450,001–600,000	19.92
600,001–750,000	26.68
750,001–900,000	26.03
900,001 and above	23.15

From *Ergebnissen über die Produktionsverhältnisse des Mühlengewerbes*, compiled by the Department of the Interior (Berlin, 1913).

III

Theoretical assumptions and nonobserved facts

Economics today rides the crest of intellectual respectability and popular acclaim. The serious attention with which our pronouncements are received by the general public, hard-bitten politicians, and even skeptical businessmen is second only to that which was given to physicists and space experts a few years ago when the round trip to the moon seemed to be our only truly national goal. The flow of learned articles, monographs, and textbooks is swelling like a tidal wave; *Econometrica*, the leading journal in the field of mathematical economics, has just stepped up its publication schedule from four to six issues per annum.

And yet an uneasy feeling about the present state of our discipline has been growing in some of us who have watched its unprecedented development over the last three decades. This concern seems to be shared even by those who are themselves contributing successfully to the present boom. They play the game with professional skill but have serious doubts about its rules.

Much of current academic teaching and research has been criticized for its lack of relevance, that is, of immediate practical impact. In a nearly instant response to this criticism, research projects, seminars, and undergraduate courses have been set up on poverty, on city and small town slums, on pure water and fresh air. In an almost Pavlovian reflex, whenever a new complaint is raised,

Presidential address delivered at the eighty-third meeting of the American Economic Association, Detroit, Michigan, December 29, 1970; published in *The American Economic Review*, Vol. 61, 1971.

President Nixon appoints a commission and the university announces a new course. Far be it from me to argue that the fire should not be shifted when the target moves. The trouble is caused, however, not by an inadequate selection of targets, but rather by our inability to hit squarely any one of them. The uneasiness of which I spoke before is caused not by the *irrelevance* of the practical problems to which present-day economists address their efforts, but rather by the palpable *inadequacy* of the scientific means with which they try to solve them.

If this simply were a sign of the overly high aspiration level of a fast developing discipline, such a discrepancy between ends and means should cause no worry. But I submit that the consistently indifferent performance in practical applications is in fact a symptom of a fundamental imbalance in the present state of our discipline. The weak and all too slowly growing empirical foundation clearly cannot support the proliferating superstructure of pure, or should I say, speculative economic theory.

Much is being made of the widespread, nearly mandatory use by modern economic theorists of mathematics. To the extent to which the economic phenomena possess observable quantitative dimensions, this is indisputably a major forward step. Unfortunately, anyone capable of learning elementary, or preferably advanced calculus and algebra, and acquiring acquaintance with the specialized terminology of economics can set himself up as a theorist. Uncritical enthusiasm for mathematical formulation tends often to conceal the ephemeral substantive content of the argument behind the formidable front of algebraic signs.

Professional journals have opened wide their pages to papers written in mathematical language; colleges train aspiring young economists to use this language; graduate schools require its knowledge and reward its use. The mathematical-model-building industry has grown into one of the most prestigious, possibly the most prestigious branch of economics. Construction of a typical theoretical model can be handled now as a routine assembly job. All principal components such as production functions, consumption and utility functions come in several standard types; so does the optional equipment as, for example, "factor augmentation"—to take care of technological change. This particular device is, incidentally, available in a simple exponential design or with a special automatic regulator known as the "Kennedy function." Any model can be modernized with the help of special attachments. One popular way to upgrade a simple one-sector model is to bring it out in a two-sector version or even in a still more impressive form of the "n-sector," that is, many-sector class.

In the presentation of a new model, attention nowadays is usually centered on a step-by-step derivation of its formal properties. But if the author—or at least the referee who recommended the manuscript for publication—is technically competent, such mathematical manipulations, however long and intricate, can even without further checking be accepted as correct. Nevertheless, they are usually spelled out at great length. By the time it comes to interpretation of the substantive *conclusions*, the assumptions on which the model has been based are easily forgotten. But it is precisely the empirical validity of these *assumptions* on which the usefulness of the entire exercise depends.

What is really needed, in most cases, is a very difficult and seldom very neat assessment and verification of these assumptions in terms of observed facts. Here mathematics cannot help, and because of this, the interest and enthusiasm of the model builder suddenly begins to flag: "If you do not like my set of assumptions, give me another and I will gladly make you another model; have your pick."

Policy-oriented models, in contrast to purely descriptive ones, are gaining favor, however nonoperational they may be. This, I submit, is in part because the choice of the final policy objectives—the selection and justification of the shape of the so-called objective function—is, and rightly so, considered based on normative judgment, not on factual analysis. Thus, the model builder can secure at least some convenient assumptions without running the risk of being asked to justify them on empirical grounds.

To sum up with the words of a recent president of the Econometric Society, " . . . the achievements of economic theory in the last two decades are both impressive and in many ways beautiful. But it cannot be denied that there is something scandalous in the spectacle of so many people refining the analysis of economic states which they give no reason to suppose will ever, or have ever, come about. . . . It is an unsatisfactory and slightly dishonest state of affairs."

But shouldn't this harsh judgment be suspended in the face of the impressive volume of econometric work? The answer is decidedly no.

This work can be in general characterized as an attempt to compensate for the glaring weakness of the data base available to us by the widest possible use of more and more sophisticated statistical techniques. Alongside the mounting pile of elaborate theoretical models we see a fast-growing stock of equally intricate statistical tools. These are intended to stretch to the limit the meager supply of facts.

Since, as I said before, the publishers' referees do a competent job, most model-testing kits described in professional journals are internally consistent. However, like the economic models they are supposed to implement, the validity of these statistical tools depends itself on the acceptance of certain convenient assumptions pertaining to stochastic properties of the phenomena which the particular models are intended to explain—assumptions that can be seldom verified.

In no other field of empirical inquiry has so massive and sophisticated a statistical machinery been used with such indifferent results. Nevertheless, theorists continue to turn out model after model and mathematical statisticians to devise complicated procedures one after another. Most of these are relegated to the stockpile without any practical application or after only a perfunctory demonstration exercise. Even those used for a while soon fall out of favor, not because the methods that supersede them perform better, but because they are new and different.

Continued preoccupation with imaginary, hypothetical, rather than with observable reality has gradually led to a distortion of the informal valuation scale used in our academic community to assess and to rank the scientific performance of its members. Empirical analysis, according to this scale, gets a lower rating than formal mathematical reasoning. Devising a new statistical procedure, however tenuous, that makes it possible to squeeze out one more unknown parameter from a given set of data, is judged a greater scientific achievement than the successful search for additional information that would permit us to measure the magnitude of the same parameter in a less ingenious, but more reliable way. This despite the fact that in all too many instances sophisticated statistical analysis is performed on a set of data whose exact meaning and validity are unknown to the author or, rather, so well known to him that at the very end he warns the reader not to take the material conclusions of the entire "exercise" seriously.

A natural Darwinian feedback operating through selection of

academic personnel contributes greatly to the perpetuation of this state of affairs. The scoring system that governs the distribution of rewards must naturally affect the makeup of the competing teams. Thus, it is not surprising that the younger economists, particularly those engaged in teaching and in academic research, seem by now quite content with a situation in which they can demonstrate their prowess (and, incidentally, advance their careers) by building more and more complicated mathematical models and devising more and more sophisticated methods of statistical inference without ever engaging in empirical research. Complaints about the lack of indispensable primary data are heard from time to time, but they don't sound very urgent. The feeling of dissatisfaction with the present state of our discipline which prompts me to speak out so bluntly seems, alas, to be shared by relatively few. Yet even those few who do share it feel they can do little to improve the situation. How could they?

In contrast to most physical sciences, we study a system that is not only exceedingly complex but is also in a state of constant flux. I have in mind not the obvious change in the variables, such as outputs, prices, or levels of employment, that our equations are supposed to explain, but the basic structural relationships described by the form and the parameters of these equations. In order to know what the shape of these structural relationships actually is at any given time, we have to keep them under continuous surveillance.

By sinking the foundations of our analytical system deeper and deeper, by reducing, for example, cost functions to production functions and the production functions to some still more basic relationships eventually capable of explaining the technological change itself, we should be able to reduce this drift. It would, nevertheless, be quite unrealistic to expect to reach, in this way, the bedrock of invariant structural relationships (measurable parameters) which, once having been observed and described, could be used year after year, decade after decade, without revisions based on repeated observation.

On the relatively shallow level where the empirically implemented economic analysis now operates even the more invariant of the structural relationships, in terms of which the system is described, change rapidly. Without a constant inflow of new data the existing stock of factual information becomes obsolete very soon. What a contrast with physics, biology, or even psychology, where the magnitude of most parameters is practically constant and where critical experiments and measurements don't have to be repeated every year!

Just to keep up our very modest current capabilities we have to maintain a steady flow of new data. A progressive expansion of these capabilities would be out of the question without a continuous and rapid rise of this flow. Moreover, the new, additional data in many instances will have to be qualitatively different from those provided hitherto.

To deepen the foundation of our analytical system it will be necessary to reach unhesitatingly beyond the limits of the domain of economic phenomena as it has been staked out up to now. The pursuit of a more fundamental understanding of the process of production inevitably leads into the area of engineering sciences. To penetrate below the skin-thin surface of conventional consumption functions, it will be necessary to develop a systematic study of the structural characteristics and of the functioning of households, an area in which description and analysis of social, anthropological, and demographic factors must obviously occupy the center of the stage.

Establishment of systematic cooperative relationships across the traditional frontiers now separating economics from these adjoining fields is hampered by the sense of self-sufficiency resulting from what I have already characterized as undue reliance on indirect statistical inference as the principal method of empirical research. As theorists, we construct systems in which prices, outputs, rates of saving and investment, etc., are explained in terms of production functions, consumption functions, and other structural relationships whose parameters are assumed, at least for argument's sake, to be known. As econometricians, engaged in what passes for empirical research, we do not try, however, to ascertain the actual shapes of these functions and to measure the magnitudes of these parameters by turning up new factual information. We make an about face and rely on indirect statistical inference to derive the unknown structural relationships from the observed magnitudes of prices, outputs, and other variables that, in our role as theoreticians, we treated as unknowns.

Formally, nothing is, of course, wrong with such an apparently circular procedure. Moreover, the model builder, in erecting his hypothetical structures, is free to take into account all possible kinds of factual knowledge and the econometrician, in principle, at least, can introduce in the estimating procedure any amount of what is usually referred to as "exogenous" information before he feeds his programmed tape into the computer. Such options are exercised rarely and, when they are, usually in a casual way.

The same well-known sets of figures are used again and again in all possible combinations to pit different theoretical models against each other in formal statistical combat. For obvious reasons a decision is reached in most cases not by a knock-out, but by a few points. The orderly and systematic nature of the entire procedure generates a feeling of comfortable self-sufficiency.

This complacent feeling, as I said before, discourages venturesome attempts to widen and to deepen the empirical foundations of economic analysis, particularly those attempts that would involve crossing the conventional lines separating ours from the adjoining fields.

True advance can be achieved only through an iterative process in which improved theoretical formulation raises new empirical questions and the answers to these questions, in their turn, lead to new theoretical insights. The "givens" of today become the "unknowns" that will have to be explained tomorrow. This, incidentally, makes untenable the admittedly convenient methodological position according to which a theorist does not need to verify directly the factual assumptions on which he chooses to base his deductive arguments, provided his empirical conclusions seem to be correct. The prevalence of such a point of view is, to a large extent, responsible for the state of splendid isolation in which our discipline nowadays finds itself.

An exceptional example of a healthy balance between theoretical and empirical analysis and of the readiness of professional economists to cooperate with experts in the neighboring disciplines is offered by agricultural economics as it developed in this country over the last fifty years. A unique combination of social and political forces has secured for this area unusually strong organizational and generous financial support. Official agricultural statistics are more complete, reliable, and systematic than those pertaining to any other major sector of our economy. Close collaboration with agronomists provides agricultural economists with direct access to information of a technological kind. When they speak of crop rotation, fertilizers, or alternative harvesting techniques, they usually know, sometimes from personal experience, what they are talking about. Preoccupation with the standard of living of the rural population has led agricultural economists into collaboration with home economists and sociologists, that is, with social scientists of the "softer" kind. While centering their interest on only one part of the economic system, agricultural economists demonstrated the effectiveness of a systematic combination of theoretical approach with detailed factual analysis. They also were the first among economists to make use of the advanced methods of mathematical statistics. However, in their hands, statistical inference became a complement to, not a substitute for, empirical research.

The shift from casual empiricism that dominates much of today's econometric work to systematic large-scale factual analysis will not be easy. To start with, it will require a sharp increase in the annual appropriation for federal statistical agencies. The quality of government statistics has, of course, been steadily improving. The coverage, however, does not keep up with the growing complexity of our social and economic system and our capability of handling larger and larger data flows.

The spectacular advances in computer technology increased the economists' potential ability to make effective analytical use of large sets of detailed data. The time is past when the best that could be done with large sets of variables was to reduce their number by averaging them out or, what is essentially the same, combining them into broad aggregates; now we can manipulate complicated analytical systems without suppressing the identity of their individual elements. There is a certain irony in the fact that, next to the fast-growing service industries, the areas whose coverage by the Census is particularly deficient are the operations of government agencies, both federal and local.

To place all or even the major responsibility for the collection of economic data in the hands of one central organization would be a mistake. The prevailing decentralized approach that permits and encourages a great number of government agencies, nonprofit institutions, and private businesses engaged in data-gathering activities acquitted itself very well. Better information means more detailed information, and detailed specialized information can be best collected by those immediately concerned with a particular field. What is urgently needed, however, is the establishment, maintenance, and enforcement of coordinated uniform classification systems by all agencies, private as well as public, involved in this work. Incompatible data are useless data. How far from a tolerable, not to say ideal, state our present economic statistics are in in this respect can be judged by the fact that, because of differences in classification, domestic output data cannot be compared, for many goods, with the corresponding export and import figures. Neither can the official employment statistics be related without laborious adjustments to output data, industry by industry. An unreasonably high proportion of material and intellectual resources devoted to statistical work is now spent not on the collection of primary information but on a frustrating and wasteful struggle with incongruous definitions and irreconcilable classifications.

Without invoking a misplaced methodological analogy, the task of securing a massive flow of primary economic data can be compared to that of providing the high-energy physicists with a gigantic accelerator. The scientists have their machines while the economists are still waiting for their data. In our case not only must the society be willing to provide year after year the millions of dollars required for maintenance of a vast statistical machine, but a large number of citizens must be prepared to play, at least, a passive and occasionally even an active part in actual fact-finding operations. It is as if the electrons and protons had to be persuaded to cooperate with the physicist.

The average American does not seem to object to being interviewed, polled, and surveyed. Curiosity, the desire to find out how the economic system (in which most of us are small gears, and some, big wheels) works might in many instances provide sufficient inducement for cooperation of this kind.

One runs up occasionally, of course, against the attitude that "what you don't know can't hurt you" and that knowledge might be dangerous: it may generate a desire to tinker with the system. The experience of these years seems, however, to have convinced not only most economists—with a few notable exceptions—but also the public at large that a lack of economic knowledge can hurt badly. Our free enterprise system has rightly been compared to a gigantic computing machine capable of solving its own problems automatically. But anyone who has had some practical experience with large computers knows that they do break down and can't operate unattended. To keep the automatic, or rather the semiautomatic, engine of our economy in good working order we must not only understand the general principles on which it operates, but also be acquainted with the details of its actual design.

A new element has entered the picture in recent years—the adoption of methods of modern economic analysis by private business. Corporate support of economic research goes as far back as the early 1920s when Wesley Mitchell founded the National Bureau. However, it is not this concern for broad issues of public policies or even the general interest in economic growth and business fluctuations that I have in mind, but rather the fast-spreading use of advanced methods of operations research and of so-called systems analysis. Some of the standard concepts and analytical devices of economic theory first found their way into the curricula of our business schools and soon after that, sophisticated management began to put them into practice. While academic theorists are content with the formulation of general principles, corporate operations researchers and practical systems analysts have to answer questions pertaining to specific real situations. Demand for economic data to be used in practical business planning is growing at an accelerated pace. It is a high-quality demand: business users in most instances possess first-hand technical knowledge of the area to which the data they ask for refer. Moreover, this demand is usually "effective." Profit-making business is willing and able to pay the costs of gathering the information it wants to have. This raises the thorny question of public access to privately collected data and of the proper division of labor and cooperation between government and business in that fast-expanding field. Under the inexorable pressure of rising practical demand, these problems will be solved in one way or another. Our economy will be surveyed and mapped in all its many dimensions on a larger and larger scale.

Economists should be prepared to take a leading role in shaping this major social enterprise not as someone else's spokesmen and advisers, but on their own behalf. They have failed to do this up to now. The Conference of Federal Statistics Users organized several years ago had business, labor, and many other groups represented among its members, but not economists as such. How can we expect our needs to be satisfied if our voices are not heard?

We, I mean the academic economists, are ready to expound, to anyone ready to lend an ear, our views on problems of public policy: give advice on the best ways to maintain full employment, to fight inflation, to foster economic growth. We should be equally prepared to share with the wider public the hopes and disappointments which accompany the advance of our own often desperately difficult, but always exciting intellectual enterprise. This public has amply demonstrated its readiness to back the pursuit of knowledge. It will lend its generous support to our venture too, if we take the trouble to explain what it is all about.

Reference

F. H. Hahn, "Some Adjustment Problems," *Econometrica*, Jan. 1970, 38, 1–2.

IV

An alternative to aggregation in input-output analysis and national accounts

I

The schematic uniformity of standard input-output computations accounts for certain practical advantages of that approach as well as for some of its peculiar limitations. One of the principal advantages of such uniformity is the opportunity it offers for using the matrix of technical coefficients, A, as a central storage bin for the basic factual information used again and again in various computations.

A comparison of the structural properties of two economies—or of the structural characteristics of the same economy at two different points of time—is reduced in this context to a comparison of two A matrices. The only (and admittedly very serious) difficulty arising in any attempt to ascertain the differences and similarities between the magnitudes of individual technical coefficients—or of the whole rows, or entire columns of such coefficients—in two matrices is often caused by the incomparability of the sectoral breakdown in terms of which the two tables were originally compiled.

These differences might turn out to be of a merely terminological or classificatory kind. This means that, in principle, at least, with full access to all the basic facts and figures, new matrices could be constructed that would describe the two essentially comparable

From *The Review of Economics and Statistics*, Vol. 49, No. 3, August 1967.

I want to express my thanks to the staff of the Harvard Economic Research Project and particularly to Mrs. Brookes Byrd for the indispensable assistance in the preparation of the material presented in this paper. Frankly, the responsibility for the minor errors that might have crept into it rests with them.

economic structures in appropriately comparable terms.

The lack of perfect correspondence between the sectoral headings of two input-output tables might, however, frequently reflect the presence in one of the two economies of some goods or services that are neither produced nor consumed in the other. In this instance, reclassification will not help. In the extreme, albeit most unlikely, case in which the two economies have no goods or services in common, the very thought of structural comparison would have to be given up.

More often, when all the justifiable preliminary realignments of the original classifications have been made, the two matrices will turn out to have some reasonably comparable sectors, while some of the other sectors contained in one of them will have no matching counterparts in the other. Even when such incomparability is known to be due only to differences in the commodity and industry classifications used, the figures entered in those rows and columns must be treated as describing structures of incomparable kinds.

In current statistical practice, the solution of the difficulties described above is sought in aggregation. The difference between copper and nickel vanishes as soon as both are treated as "nonferrous metals" and both become indistinguishable from steel as soon as the qualifying specification "nonferrous" has been dropped too. The fact that comparability through aggregation is secured at the cost of analytical sharpness in the description of the underlying structural relationships is too well known to require explanation.

The method of double inversion described below permits us to reduce to a common denominator two input-output matrices that contain some comparable and also some incomparable sectors. In contrast to conventional aggregation, such analytical reduction is achieved without distortion of any of the basic structural relationships. The comparability of input-output tables attained through double inversion is limited in the sense that their respective structures are described only in terms of input-output relationships between goods and services of directly comparable kinds. It is, nevertheless, an overall comparability to the extent that all the structural characteristics of each of the two systems, including the magnitudes of the technical coefficients located in the "incomparable" rows and columns, are taken into account fully without omission or distortion.

II

To facilitate the intuitive understanding of the transformation that leads to the construction of what might be called a reduced input-output matrix of a national economy, we will ask the reader to visualize a situation in which—for trading purposes—all industries of a country have been divided into two groups. The industries belonging to group I are identified as the "contracting," those in group II as the "subcontracting," industries.

Each contracting, i.e., group I industry covers its direct input requirements for the products of other group I industries by direct purchases, and each group II industry makes direct purchases from other group II industries. However, the products of group II industries delivered to group I industries are manufactured on the basis of special work contracts. Under such a contract, the group I industry placing an order with a group II industry provides the latter with the products of all group I industries (including its own), in amounts required to fill that particular order. To be able to do so, it purchases all these goods—from the group I industries that make them—on its own account. The relationship between a contracting (group I) and a subcontracting (group II) industry is thus analogous to the relationship between a customer who buys the cloth himself and the tailor who makes it up for him into a suit.

In determining the amounts of goods and services that he will have to purchase from his own and all the other group I industries, the procurement officer of each group I industry will have to add to the immediate input requirements of his own sector the amounts to be processed for it—under contract—by various group II industries. For all practical purposes, such augmented shopping lists now constitute the effective input vectors of all the group I industries.

The square array of n_1 such column vectors—each containing n_1 elements (some of which may of course be zero)—represents the reduced table of input coefficients that we seek. It describes the same system as the original table; however, it describes it only in terms of goods and services produced by the selected contracting industries included in group I.

The relationship between the two tables is similar to the relationship of an abbreviated timetable that lists only selected large stations to the complete detailed timetable that also shows all the intermediate stops. The subdivision of all the sectors of an economy into groups I and II must, of course, depend on the specific purpose that the consolidated system is intended to serve.

Using a reduced table for planning purposes, we can be sure that if the input-output flows among the group I industries shown in it are properly balanced, the balance between the outputs and inputs of all the group II industries omitted from it will be secured, too.

In the process of consolidation, the allocation of so-called primary inputs will change, as well. The new labor and capital coefficients of each group I industry must now reflect not only its own immediate labor and capital requirements, but also the labor and capital requirements of all the group II industries from which it draws some of its supplies. It is as if, under the imaginary contractual arrangements described above, each group I industry had to provide the group II industries working for it, not only with the goods and services produced by any of the group I sectors, but also with all the capital and labor required by these group II industries to fulfill these contracts. Thus, the output levels of all the group I industries, as projected on the basis of a reduced input-output table (multiplied with the appropriate consolidated capital and labor coefficients), will account not only for the capital and labor requirements of these group I industries, but also for those of all the group II industries without whose support these output levels could not have been attained.

III

Not unlike conventional aggregation, the analytical procedure described below is aimed at a reduction of the number of sectors in terms of which the particular economic structure was originally described. It is, however, a "clean"—not an index number—operation. It does not involve introduction of weights or any other arbitrary constants.

Equation (1) describes—in conventional matrix notation—the relationships between the total output vector, X, of all the sectors of a particular economy, and the corresponding final bill of goods, Y.

$$(1) \qquad\qquad (I - A) X = Y.$$

In equation (2), both vectors are split into two parts: the column vectors X_1 and Y_1 represent the total outputs and the final deliveries of group I industries that produce the n_1 goods that will be retained in the reduced matrix, while X_2 and Y_2 represent the outputs and the final deliveries of all the other, i.e., the n_2, goods produced by the group II industries that have to be eliminated.

$$(2) \qquad \begin{bmatrix} (I - A_{11}) & -A_{12} \\ -A_{21} & (I - A_{22}) \end{bmatrix} \begin{bmatrix} X_1 \\ X_2 \end{bmatrix} = \begin{bmatrix} Y_1 \\ Y_2 \end{bmatrix}.$$

The matrix $(I - A)$ on the left-hand side is partitioned, in conformity with the output vector into which it is multiplied. A_{11} and A_{22} are square matrices whose elements are technical coefficients that govern the internal flows between the sectors of the first and of the second groups, respectively, while A_{12} and A_{21} are rectangular (not necessarily square) matrices describing the direct requirements of industries of the second group for outputs of the first group and vice versa.

Equation (3) is the solution of (2) for X in terms of Y.

$$(3) \qquad \begin{bmatrix} X_1 \\ X_2 \end{bmatrix} = \begin{bmatrix} B_{11} & B_{12} \\ B_{21} & B_{22} \end{bmatrix} \begin{bmatrix} Y_1 \\ Y_2 \end{bmatrix}.$$

Matrix B is the *inverse* of $(I - A)$. It is partitioned in conformity with the partitioning of $(I - A)$ in equation (2). After the multiplication has been carried out on its right-hand side, equation (3) can be split in two:

$$(4) \qquad X_1 = B_{11}Y_1 + B_{12}Y_2$$

$$(5) \qquad X_2 = B_{21}Y_1 + B_{22}Y_2.$$

Premultiplying both sides of (4) by B_{11}^{-1}, we have:

$$(6) \qquad B_{11}^{-1}X_1 = Y_1 + B_{11}^{-1}B_{12}Y_2.$$

This equation can be interpreted as a reduced version of the original system (2). It describes the same structural relationships; however, it represents them only in terms of the goods and services produced by the n_1 industries assigned to group I. The variables contained in vector X_2—that is, the outputs of the n_2 industries assigned to group II—have been eliminated by means of two successive matrix inversions that led from (2) to (6).

Let a new structural matrix and a new final demand vector be defined by:

$$(7) \qquad A_{11}{}^* = I - B_{11}{}^{-1}$$

$$(8) \qquad Y_1{}^* = Y_1 + B_{11}{}^{-1}B_{12}Y_2.$$

In this notation (6) can be rewritten as:

$$(9) \qquad (I - A_{11}{}^*)X_1 = Y_1{}^*.$$

In perfect analogy with the original system (1) this equation describes the input-output relationships between the redefined vector of final deliveries, $Y_1{}^*$, and the corresponding vector of total outputs X_1.[1] Solved for X_1 in terms of $Y_1{}^*$, it yields:

$$(10) \qquad X_1 = (I - A_{11}{}^*)^{-1}Y_1{}^*.$$

This equation is, of course, formally equivalent to (4). $A_{11}{}^*$ is the structural matrix of the economy that was originally described by A. However, the same structure is now described in terms of the n_1 group I industries alone. The first column of $A_{11}{}^*$ consists, for example, of n_1 technical coefficients, $a_{11}{}^*$, $a_{21}{}^*$, . . . , $a_{n1}{}^*$, showing the number of units of each of these n_1 industries of group I required per unit of the total output, x_1, of the first. Although not referring to them explicitly, implicitly these coefficients reflect the input requirements also of the other n_2 industries eliminated in the reduction process.

Let, for example, industry 1 produce "steel" and industry 2, "electric energy," both assigned to group I. In the reduced matrix $A_{11}{}^*$, the coefficient $a_{21}{}^*$ thus represents the number of kilowatt-hours (or a dollar's worth) of electricity required to produce a ton (or a dollar's worth) of steel. This requirement is computed to cover not only the direct deliveries of electricity from generating stations to steel plants, but also the indirect deliveries channeled through industries assigned to group II. If "iron mining" were, for instance, considered as belonging to group II, the electricity used in extraction and preparation of the iron ore that went into the production of one ton (or a dollar's worth) of steel would also be included in the input coefficient $a_{21}{}^*$, and so would electric power absorbed by the steel industry via all other sectors assigned to group II.

[1] The symbol $X_1{}^*$ is not used because the reduced system has been derived in such a way that $X_1 \equiv X_1{}^*$.

In other words, the array of the input coefficients (with asterisks) that make up the first column of matrix $A_{11}{}^*$ describes the combination of the products of industries included in group I with which the economy in question would be capable of turning out a ton (or a dollar's worth) of steel. Some of these inputs reach the steel industry indirectly through industries assigned to group II.

The reduced structural matrix $A_{11}{}^*$ describes explicitly only the input structure of the group I industries and this only in terms of their own products. Implicitly, it reflects, nevertheless, the technological characteristics of all the other industries as well. The relationship between elements of the reduced and the original matrix is displayed clearly if $A_{11}{}^*$ is expressed directly in terms of the elements of the partitioned matrix A:[2]

$$(11) \qquad A_{11}{}^* = A_{11} + A_{12}(I - A_{22})^{-1}A_{21}.$$

The well-known sufficient conditions for the ability of the given input-output system to maintain—without drawing on outside help—a positive level of final consumption, i.e., to possess a positive inverse $(I - A)^{-1}$, requires that none of the column (or row) totals of the technical coefficients in A_{11} exceed one, and at least one of these sum totals be less than one. This implies that the inverse $(I - A)^{-1}$ is nonnegative. All the components of the second term on the right-hand side of (11) being either zero or positive, each element $a_{ij}{}^*$ of the consolidated structural matrix has to be either equal to, or larger than, the corresponding originally given input coefficient, a_{ij}.

The final deliveries on the right-hand side of the reduced system (6) are composed of two parts. Vector Y_1 is the demand for the products of the group I industries as it appears in the original system (2). Vector $B_{11}{}^{-1}B_{12}Y_2$ $(\equiv A_{12}(I - A_{22})^{-1}Y_2)$ represents the final demand for the products of the second group of goods translated into the requirements for inputs of goods belonging to the first. In the special case in

---

[2] Since $B = (I - A)^{-1}$,
$$B(I - A) = I.$$
In particular:
$$B_{11}(I - A_{11}) - B_{12}A_{21} = I$$
$$-B_{11}A_{12} + B_{12}(I - A_{22}) = 0.$$
Eliminating B_{12} and rearranging yields:
$$A_{11}{}^* = I - B_{11}{}^{-1} = A_{11} + A_{12}(I - A_{22})^{-1}A_{21}.$$

which the final users happen to demand directly only commodities and services of group I, while group II consists exclusively of intermediate goods, Y_2 vanishes and, save for the omission of its zero components, the final deliveries vector of the original system would enter without any change into the smaller, reduced system, too.

IV

A primary input, such as labor, a natural resource, or—in a static system—a stock of some kind of capital goods, can be treated in the process of reduction as if it were a product of a separate industry included in group I.

The row assigned to each primary factor in the original matrix A will contain the appropriate technical input coefficients: labor coefficients, capital coefficients, and so on. The columns corresponding to these rows will consist of zeros, since, in contrast to other goods and services, the output of a primary factor is not considered to be formally dependent on inputs originating in other industries.[3]

The labor, capital, and other primary factor coefficients appearing in the appropriate rows of matrix A^* will never be smaller—and in most instances they will be larger—than the corresponding elements of the original matrix A. As all the other input coefficients in the reduced system, they cover not only the immediate requirements of each group I industry, but also the labor and capital employed by group II industries (eliminated in the process of analytical reduction) from which that industry receives all its group II supplies.

V

Any static input-output system implies the existence of linear relationships between the prices of all products and the "value added" in all the sectors per unit of their respective outputs.[4] While a reduction of a structural matrix eliminates some of the prices from the picture, it

[3] The matrix $(I - A)$ is nevertheless not singular: its main diagonal contains positive elements throughout.
[4] The "value added" in any industry can, in its turn, be described as a sum of the input coefficients of all factors multiplied by their respective prices augmented by the amount of positive or negative net surplus earned per unit of its output.

leaves the relationship between the remaining prices and the values added essentially intact.

Let P be the price vector of the original system and V the vector of values added per unit of output in its n different sectors. The basic relationships between the two vectors,

$$(12) \qquad\qquad (I - A') P = V$$

can be solved for the unknown prices in terms of given values added:

$$(13) \qquad\qquad \begin{bmatrix} P_1 \\ \hline P_2 \end{bmatrix} = \begin{bmatrix} B_{11}' & \vdots & -B_{21}' \\ \hline B_{12}' & \vdots & -B_{22}' \end{bmatrix} \begin{bmatrix} V_1 \\ \hline -V_2 \end{bmatrix}.$$

The "primes" above the B's indicate transposition, i.e., permutation of rows and columns. The partitioning of the two vectors and of the structural matrix corresponds to a similar partitioning in (3) above. Solving for P_1 we have:

$$(14) \qquad\qquad P_1 = B_{11}'V_1{}^*, \text{ where}$$

$$(15) \qquad\qquad V_1{}^* = V_1 + (B_{11}')^{-1}B_{21}'V_2.$$

The last equation shows that, analogous to the reduced final bill of goods, $Y_1{}^*$, in (8), $V_1{}^*$ represents the augmented values added vector of the group I industries. Each element of that augmented vector contains not only the value added—shown for each one of them in the original table—but also the value added in group II industries imputed through all the goods and services which the particular group I sector receives from them. In view of (7), (14) can be rewritten as:

$$(16) \qquad\qquad P_1 = (I - A^{*\prime})^{-1}V_1{}^*.$$

Inserting on the right-hand side the augmented values added in group I industries, we obtain on the left-hand side a set of prices identical with those that would have been derived from group I outputs from the original (unreduced) set of price equations (13–15).

VI

A recently completed study of metalworking industries called for analysis of interdependence among the several branches of production belonging to this group, and for an assessment of its position within the United States national economy as a whole. Of the 73 producing sectors in the 1958 input-output table,[5] 23 are making or transforming metals; 5 of them supply intermediate ferrous or nonferrous products, while the other 18 are engaged in the manufacture of basic materials and finished metal goods.

The immediate technical interdependence among the 23 metalworking sectors is reflected in the magnitude of the input coefficients located on the intersections of the 23 rows and the corresponding 23 columns in the large 73-sector table mentioned above.

The production of the nonmetal inputs absorbed by metalworking industries often requires the use of various metal products in its turn. The dependence of each metalworking sector upon all the others (taking into account such indirect requirements) is described by the augmented input coefficients entered in the 23 rows and columns of the reduced matrix that was obtained through analytical elimination of all the 50 nonmetalworking sectors from the original table. The full interdependence between the 18 metalworking industries engaged in the manufacture of raw and finished metal products can be brought out through further reduction that eliminates from the large table also the five intermediate metalworking industries.

A row of labor coefficients, and another of (total) capital coefficients, was added at the outset to the original 73-sector matrix. After reduction, appropriately augmented labor and capital coefficients appeared in the last two rows of both reduced matrices as well.

In Table 1, the technical coefficients describing the inputs of various metal products required by the "motor vehicles and equipment" industry, as they appear in the original 73-sector matrix, are shown in column (1). The second column contains the corresponding augmented coefficients, as they appear in the reduced matrix composed of the 23 metalworking sectors. The third column shows the 18 still more augmented coefficients as they appear in the motor vehicles and equipment column of a reduced matrix, from which the five basic metalworking industries were eliminated too. Appropriate labor and capital coefficients are entered at the bottom of all three columns.

[5] U.S. Department of Commerce, *Survey of Current Business*, 44, No. 11 (Nov. 1964); and Anne P. Carter, "Changes in the Structure of the American Economy, 1947 to 1958 and 1962," *Review of Economics and Statistics*, XLIX (May 1967).

SECTOR NUMBER THE 73-SECTOR MATRIX	INDUSTRY	INPUT COEFFICIENTS IN THE		
		ORIGINAL 73-SECTOR MATRIX[b]	REDUCED 23-SECTOR MATRIX[c]	REDUCED 18-SECTOR MATRIX
59	Motor vehicles and equipment	0.29757	0.29817	0.29991
37	Primary iron and steel manufacturing	0.08780	0.08874	0.10714
42	Other fabricated metal products	0.03603	0.03713	
41	Screw machine products, bolts, nuts, etc., metal stamping	0.03103	0.03137	
47	General industrial and metalworking machinery, and equipment	0.02364	0.02456	
58	Miscellaneous electrical machinery equipment and supplies	0.01543	0.01557	0.01564
38	Primary nonferrous metals manufacturing	0.01144	0.01205	0.01871
56	Radio, television, and communication equipment	0.00523	0.00557	0.00576
62	Professional, scientific, and control instruments and supplies	0.00438	0.00460	0.00498
55	Electric lighting and wiring equipment	0.00420	0.00441	0.00475
43	Engines and turbines	0.00379	0.00402	0.00437
53	Electrical industrial equipment	0.00217	0.00236	
52	Service industrial machinery, household appliances	0.00129	0.00157	0.00208
44	Farm machinery and equipment	0.00105	0.00129	0.00144
40	Heating, plumbing, and structural metal products	0.00102	0.00147	
64	Miscellaneous manufacturing	0.00092	0.00201	0.00245
61	Transportation equipment, miscellaneous	0.00089	0.00123	0.00143
57	Electronic components and accessories	0.00079	0.00090	0.00111
45	Construction, mining, oil field machinery and equipment	0.00044	0.00062	0.00094
60	Aircraft and parts	0.00039	0.00086	0.00123
46	Materials handling machinery and equipment	0.00022	0.00027	0.00046
63	Optical, ophthalmic, photographic equipment	0.00005	0.00045	0.00053
51	Office, computing and accounting machines	0.00000	0.00069	0.00079
	Labor	0.02645	0.04729	0.05614
	Capital stock	0.24313	0.47495	0.55890

[a]Units of measurement: for labor coefficients, man-years per $1,000 of output; for all other coefficients, 1958 dollars per dollar of output.
[b]This matrix is based on the 1958 input-output table published by the Office of Business Economics, Department of Commerce. See Anne Carter, "Changes in the Structure of the American Economy, 1947–1958, 1962," *Review of Economics and Statistics*, XLIX (May 1967). The labor coefficients are based on Jack Alterman, "Interindustry Employment Requirements," *Monthly Labor Review*, 88, No. 7 (July 1965). The capital coefficients for manufacturing sectors were obtained from Waddell, Ritz, Norton, De Witt, and Marshall K. Wood, "Capital Expansion Planning Factors, Manufacturing Industries," *National Planning Association* (Washington, D.C., April 1966). For nonmanufacturing sectors, the capital coefficients were compiled at the Harvard Economic Research Project.
[c]The sectors eliminated through the reduction procedure are those included in the 73-sector input-output table, but not represented in this column of augmented coefficients.

VII

Table 2 is an example of a reduced national input-output table. This complete, but compact, flow chart was derived from the official 1958 United States table[6] in two successive steps.

First, 34 of the 83 productive sectors of the original table were combined into eight groups. The resulting smaller 57-sector table contained these eight aggregated industries, the 49 sectors carried over from the original 83-order table, a corresponding column of final demand and a value added row.

This 57-sector table was reduced, in a second step, through elimination of all the 49 nonaggregated industries, to a compact 8-sector table. It should be noted that the figures shown in Table 2 are total flows, not input coefficients. They were obtained through multiplication of all elements of each column of the corresponding reduced coefficient matrix by the given total output figure of the industry, the input structure of which that particular column describes.

Table 2 thus depicts the structure of the American economy in terms of flows of commodities and services among eight industrial sectors, a value added row, and a column of final demand, both reduced in conformity with the rest of the table (see equation 8). Wages and salaries paid out by various sectors are, of course, included in the value added row. In addition, a separate row of labor inputs, measured in man-years, was carried along through all computations. This row is reproduced separately at the bottom of the table.

In each cell of the table, below the number describing the appropriately augmented intersectoral transaction is entered, enclosed in parentheses, another figure. This number represents the magnitude of the input—from the sector named on the left to the sector identified at the head of the column—as it appeared in the unreduced 57-sector table obtained at the end of the first step, i.e., before the 49 unaggregated sectors were eliminated from the table in the second step.

In the final demand column, the larger entries represent the augmented deliveries to households, government, and other final users, while the entries in parentheses show the corresponding figures, as

[6] U.S. Department of Commerce, *Survey of Current Business*, 45, No. 9 (Sept. 1965).

Table 2 —Input-output table of the United States economy for the year 1958 reduced to 8 from 57 producing sectors[a]

COLUMN ROW	INDUSTRY	FOOD AND DRUGS (1)	HOUSE-WARES (2)	MACHINERY (3)	TRANS. EQUIP. & CONSUM. APPL. (4)	CONSTRUC-TION (5)	METALS (6)	ENERGY (7)	CHEMICALS (8)	FINAL DEMAND	GROSS DOMESTIC OUTPUT
1	Food and Drugs	15,202 (12,468)	547 (96)	161 (11)	353 (49)	513 (17)	165 (53)	218 (62)	386 (288)	58,728 (55,320)	76,272
2	Textiles, clothing and furnishings	347 (155)	12,815 (12,692)	92 (37)	821 (636)	761 (524)	171 (47)	63 (8)	61 (38)	21,369 (20,033)	36,500
3	Machinery	430 (28)	215 (105)	2,321 (2,186)	2,061 (1,644)	1,397 (748)	819 (545)	406 (141)	200 (150)	13,385 (11,293)	21,233
4	Transportation equipment and consumer appliances	363 (29)	158 (55)	816 (691)	11,791 (11,196)	1,372 (753)	485 (101)	183 (29)	53 (5)	38,691 (32,670)	53,912
5	Construction	1,158 (235)	218 (18)	115 (26)	308 (109)	48 (8)	284 (131)	1,541 (579)	70 (6)	65,117 (56,836)	69,291
6	Metals	1,033 (46)	475 (277)	3,073 (2,631)	6,038 (4,618)	6,468 (3,650)	7,959 (7,335)	388 (110)	479 (389)	2,244 (−45)	28,158
7	Energy	2,158 (783)	652 (293)	371 (226)	805 (404)	2,774 (1,536)	1,704 (1,391)	6,888 (6,236)	1,127 (1,007)	23,851 (17,702)	40,330
8	Chemicals	1,956 (1,056)	1,030 (218)	201 (117)	475 (115)	1,218 (437)	459 (283)	713 (576)	2,500 (2,351)	3,218 (1,510)	11,770
	Value added	53,625 (22,252)	20,390 (12,844)	14,083 (10,254)	31,260 (20,677)	54,308 (28,937)	16,112 (10,509)	29,930 (15,127)	6,894 (4,674)	178,912	405,515
TOTAL		76,272	36,500	21,233	53,912	69,291	28,158	40,330	11,770	405,515	
	Labor	8,182 (2,202)	3,929 (2,808)	1,820 (1,307)	3,891 (2,467)	8,581 (4,847)	1,867 (1,155)	1,775 (1,003)	671 (403)	26,430	57,146

[a]Derived from the 83-sector table published in "Transaction Table of the 1958 Input-Output Study and Revised Direct Requirements Data," *Survey of Current Business*, 45, No. 9 (Sept. 1965). Each of the 8 sectors of the intermediate 57-sector table retained in this reduced table represents an aggregate of the following industries identified by the numbers they carry in the original 83-sector table:
(1) Food and drugs: 14,15,29; (2) textiles, clothing, furnishings: 16, 17, 18, 19, 34, 22, 23; (3) machinery (only final): 51, 44, 45, 46, 47, 48, 49, 50, 63; (4) transportation equipment and consumer appliances: 52, 54, 56, 59, 60, 61, 62; (5) construction: 11, 12; (6) metals: 37, 38; (7) energy: 31, 68; (8) chemicals: 27.
  Corresponding entries in the unreduced 57-sector table appear in parentheses. The units are man-years in the labor row and millions of dollars in all other rows.

they appeared in the 57-sector table. The first entry exceeds, in each instance, the figure in parentheses below by the amount of the particular type of goods that was absorbed in the production of those final deliveries which were eliminated from the original table. Value added in general—and labor inputs in particular—that were absorbed in this way appear now in the final demand.

VIII

The idea that, in the description of an economic system, some processes and outputs can be reduced, that is, expressed in terms of others, goes quite far back into the history of economic thought. Adam Smith discussed at length the question of whether corn should be measured in labor units required to grow it, or, on the contrary, labor measured in terms of corn that a worker needs to live. Quesnay insisted that various branches of manufacturing should be represented in his tableau only by the amounts of rough materials that they transformed into finished products.

The notion of unproductive—as contrasted with productive—labor, whose product does not deserve to be included in the grand total of national product, was still propounded by Stuart Mill. The Marxian doctrine caused the Soviet official statistician, up until recently, to exclude transportation of persons and products of many service industries from national accounts, and, in the West, the output of governmental and other public services is still often treated in the same way.

In the latter case, the elimination of the output—as contrasted with the input—of the public sector from national accounts is justified, not so much by the distinction between productive and unproductive activities, but rather by the difficulty of measuring the output of "public administration," of "education," or of "national defense."

The number of goods and services that more and more detailed observation of various processes of production and consumption would permit us to distinguish is much greater than even an input-output matrix containing many thousands of rows and columns can possibly hold. For many purposes, that number might also be larger than we would need to carry from the first stage of the analytical procedure to the last. Aggregation, i.e., summation of essentially heterogeneous quantities, is one of the two devices that the economist uses to limit the number of variables and functional relationships in terms of which he describes what he observes. The other is reduction, that is, elimination of certain goods and processes. In this paper, a systematic procedure has been presented that permits us to reduce the size of an input-output table through analytical elimination of any of its rows and columns. A less systematic, intuitive elimination of a much larger number of variables—considered to be secondary or intermediate—occurs, however, already during the collection of the primary statistical information. Thus, even a most detailed input-output table, as well as the national accounts constructed around it, can be said to present the actual economic system, not only in an aggregated, but also in a reduced form.

V

The dynamic inverse

I

The purpose of this paper is to introduce the notion of the dynamic inverse that could play a role in the empirical study of economic change analogous to the role played in static input-output analysis by the inverse of the flow coefficient matrix.

First I shall describe the open dynamic input-output system in terms of a simple set of linear equations. Next, I shall present a general solution of that system, that is, the inverse of its structural matrix. Each element of this inverse represents the combined direct and indirect inputs required from the row industry to permit an additional output of $1 million by the column industry. While in a static inverse such effects can be described by a single number, within the framework of dynamic analysis they have to be presented in a time series: as soon as capacity expansion and the corresponding invest-ment processes are introduced explicitly into the system, the inputs contributing directly or indirectly to the delivery of a certain final output in a given year must be dated too. These come out of the computer as a sequence of numbers stretched back in time. The last sections of this paper are devoted to a brief discussion of the corres-ponding dynamic price system.[1]

From A. P. Carter and A. Brody (eds.), *Contributions to Input-Output Analysis* (Amsterdam: North-Holland Publishing Company, 1970), pp. 17–46.

In preparation of this paper the author was assisted by Brookes Byrd, Richard Berner, and Peter Petri.

[1] Basic concepts, the industry classification system, and the sources of data used in the study are presented in appendices II, III, and IV.

II

Let the column vector x represent the n sectoral outputs, $_tX_1$, $_tx_2$, . . . , $_tx_n$, produced in year t, and c the corresponding column vector, $_tc_1$, $_tc_2$, . . . , $_tc_n$, of deliveries to final demand. This final demand does *not* include the annual additions to the stock of fixed and working capital (inventories) used by the n productive sectors mentioned above. The structural characteristics of the economy are described by A_t, the square $(n \times n)$ matrix of technical flow coefficients that specifies the direct current input requirements of all industries, and B_t, the corresponding square matrix of capital coefficients. Capital goods produced in year t are assumed to be installed and put into operation in the next year, $t + 1$.

The direct interdependence between the outputs of all the sectors of a given national economy in two successive years can be described by the following familiar balance equation:

$$(1) \qquad x_t - A_t x_t - B_{t+1} (x_{t+1} - x_t) = c_t.$$

The second term on the left-hand side represents the current input requirements of all n industries in year t; the third, the investment requirements, i.e., additions to productive stock that would permit all industries to expand their capacity outputs from the year t to the next year, $t + 1$, from x_t to x_{t+1}. The time subscripts attached to both structural matrices provide the possibility of using different sets of flow and capital coefficients for different years, thus incorporating technological change into the dynamic system. It should be noted that the time subscript attached to matrix B_{t+1} identifies not the year in which the particular capital goods are produced, but rather the year in which they are first put to use. Equation (1) can be rewritten as:

$$(2) \qquad G_t x_t - B_{t+1} x_{t+1} = c_t$$

where $G_t = (1 - A_t + B_{t+1})$. A set of interlocked balance equations of this type describing the development of the given economy over a period of $m + 1$ years can be combined to form a system of $m + 1$ linear equations:

$$(3) \quad \begin{bmatrix} G_{-m} - B_{-m+1} & & & & \\ & G_{-m+1} - B_{-m+2} & & & \\ & & \ddots & \ddots & \\ & & & G_{-2} - B_{-1} & \\ & & & & G_{-1} - B_0 \\ & & & & G_0 \end{bmatrix} \begin{bmatrix} x_{-m} \\ x_{-m+1} \\ \vdots \\ x_{-2} \\ x_{-1} \\ x_0 \end{bmatrix} = \begin{bmatrix} c_{-m} \\ c_{-m+1} \\ \vdots \\ c_{-2} \\ c_{-1} \\ c_0 \end{bmatrix}$$

III

The solution of this system determines the sequence of annual total sectoral outputs that would enable the economy to yield the sequence of final annual deliveries described by the array of column vectors entered on the right-hand side. Starting with the last equation, substituting its solution into the equation next to the last and thus proceeding stepwise to the first, we arrive at the following solution of system (3) for the unknown x's in terms of a given set of the c's.

$$(4) \quad \begin{bmatrix} x_{-m} \\ \vdots \\ x_{-2} \\ x_{-1} \\ x_0 \end{bmatrix} = \begin{bmatrix} G_{-m}^{-1} \dots R_{-m} \dots R_{-3}R_{-2}G_{-1}^{-1} & R_{-m} \dots R_{-3}R_{-2}R_{-1}G_0^{-1} \\ \vdots & \vdots \\ R_{-2}G_{-1}^{-1} & R_{-2}R_{-1}G_0^{-1} \\ G_{-1}^{-1} & R_{-1}G_0^{-1} \\ & G_0^{-1} \end{bmatrix} \begin{bmatrix} c_{-m} \\ \vdots \\ c_{-2} \\ c_{-1} \\ c_0 \end{bmatrix}$$

where $R_t = G_t^{-1}B_{t+1} = (1 - A_t + B_{t+1})^{-1}B_{t+1}$.

The square matrix on the right-hand side of equation (4) is the inverse of the structural matrix that appears on the left-hand side of equation (3). Every element of this inverse is itself a square matrix.

The wedge-shaped column on the right describes the direct and indirect input requirements generated by the delivery to final demand of one unit (or one million dollars' worth) of the products of any one of the n industries in the year 0. These requirements are distributed backward over time. Matrix G_0^{-1} shows the input requirements that must be filled in year 0, i.e., the same year in which the final deliveries are made; as in a static inverse each column of G_0^{-1} identifies the industry making the delivery to final demand, each row, the industry supplying the specific input. The preceding term, $R_{-1}G_0^{-1}$, specifies the requirements that have to be filled in the preceding year -1, $R_{-2}R_{-1}G_0^{-1}$ specifies those to be filled in the year -2, and so on.

The longest term, $R_{-m} \ldots R_{-2}R_{-1}G_0^{-1}$, describes the increments in the outputs of all industries in the year $-m$, i.e., the inputs that have to be provided m years before an additional batch of goods can be delivered to final users. Each term of equation (4) located above the diagonal can be computed by multiplying the term located below it by an appropriate transformation matrix, R_{-t}.

IV

In the absence of any technical change the time subscript can be eliminated from all the structural constants. The elements of each column can in this case be described in receding order by the same simple geometric series,

$$(5) \qquad G^{-1}, \; RG^{-1}, \; R^2G^{-1}, \ldots, R^tG^{-1}, \ldots, R^mG^{-1}.$$

It is well known that as the exponent, t, becomes sufficiently large, the ratio between the magnitude of all the similarly located elements of R^t and R^{t+1} asymptotically approaches the same constant, equal to the real part of the dominant characteristic root of R. If μ is the dominant root, then $R^{t+1} \to \mathbf{R}(\mu)\, R^t$ as $t \to \infty$, where $\mathbf{R}(\mu)$ denotes the real part of the root μ. If μ is real, positive, and less than 1, the increments to outputs required to deliver any given combination of additional goods to final demand in the final year 0—traced back a sufficiently large number of years—will become smaller and smaller, and will finally become infinitely small.[2]

Thus, for all practical purposes, the chains of inputs stretching backwards from the year in which the delivery to final users is actually made, can, in case of such convergence, be treated as if they were of finite length. The same will be true even if the technical structure of the economy changes from year to year, i.e., when the R matrices retain their time subscripts. The series of required inputs converges backward in this case too, although not necessarily as smoothly as it does without technological change.

The distribution of such required inputs over time, however, varies greatly among industries. Some of the input series even dip below the

---

[2] A mathematical analysis of the convergence properties of the dynamic inverse is presented in appendix I.

zero line at their forward ends. This is the well-known effect of the so-called acceleration principle. As soon as the additional goods demanded directly or indirectly by the final users have been produced, the stocks of capital goods employed in making them will be released. The balance equation (1) is set up in such a way as to indicate negative investment, that is disinvestment, in case $x_{t+1} < x_t$. In fact such potentially idle capacity will usually be absorbed by the direct or indirect input requirements generated by increases in final deliveries scheduled for the next and subsequent years. As will be shown below these must be entered into dynamic input-output accounting in the form of separate but overlapping chains. So long as, in a given year, the sum total of positive incremental output requirements exceeds the sum total of the negative, the output of that sector will increase.

One of the analytically and operationally most useful properties of open input-output systems is the linear additivity of their solutions with respect to any changes in final demand. Each element of the final bill of goods generates a separate chain of direct and indirect input requirements. The total requirements generated by any given vector of final demand are thus represented by the sum of such chains, each corresponding to one particular component of that vector.

This remains true even if some of the separable sets have negative elements, provided the others contain corresponding positive elements large enough to yield a positive or, at least, a nonnegative sum total. In static input-output computations, competitive imports are treated, for example, as generating negative (direct and indirect) input requirements which are subtracted from the corresponding input requirements generated by the positive vector of domestic final demand, thus yielding a smaller, but still positive (or at least nonnegative) sum total. Strictly speaking, this already constitutes a departure from true separability: If that total turns out, for some particular output, to be negative, the entire result is invalidated. A new computation has to be undertaken with the imports previously treated as competitive now shifted over into the noncompetitive category. The treatment of the direct and indirect effects of one part of the final bill of goods turns out, in this case, to be dependent on the magnitude of the—admittedly separately computed—requirements generated by all the other components of that vector. This introduces into the analytical picture cross-dependencies typical of nonlinear systems.

The use of the dynamic inverse brings the obvious advantages of separability and additivity into the empirical analysis of economic change. The presence of negative elements in many of the separate input chains (describing the time sequence of the direct—but mostly indirect—input requirements generated by each individual element of a given time-phased final bill of goods) imposes obvious limits on the strict use of the additivity assumption. Consistent, i.e., feasible sequences of total input requirements can be determined on the basis of a given dynamic inverse only for those time-phased bills of goods that generate larger positive than negative output requirements for the products of each industry in each period of time.

A time-phased vector of final demand—premultiplied by a given dynamic inverse—may arithmetically yield negative total direct and indirect output requirements for some goods in some periods of time. If so, at least some of the balance equations in system (3) do not represent the real world. As everyone who has dealt with this kind of system knows, the problem arises because equation (3) assumes full capacity utilization in all the sectors all the time. By applying, for example, the simplex method routine of linear programming we could find a number of feasible production programs capable of delivering such a time-phased bill of goods. Each one of them would involve a precisely phased switching in and switching out of productive capacities and possibly the planned stockpiling of current outputs.

The operation of an economic process of such a discontinuous kind would be much more difficult to understand and to explain than that of a system whose change can be described in terms of continuous and additive components. In other words, a system with a diverging dynamic inverse that contains negative elements, whose magnitude grows as one goes back in time, could be programmed; however, the actual existence of such an economy would be very difficult to imagine. The explanation of the convergence of the actually observed dynamic inverse of the American economy which I will now describe should possibly be sought in the gradual substitution of new for the old columns of A and B coefficients, characterizing long-run technological change.

V

An open dynamic input-output system was constructed and its inverse computed on the basis of two sets of A and B matrices, one describing the structural properties of the American economy in the year 1947, the other in the year 1958. A third system was formed and inverted on the assumption that the shift from the 1947 to the 1958 technology occurred gradually over the intervening years. In all three instances the dynamic inverse turned out to be well behaved: All time series of which it consists converged backward toward zero.

The same sectoral breakdown is used for both years. It contains 52 endogenous industries and a final bill of goods subdivided into household consumption (durables and nondurables) and government consumption. An alternative treatment of private consumption separates final deliveries to households into deliveries of nondurables and of the

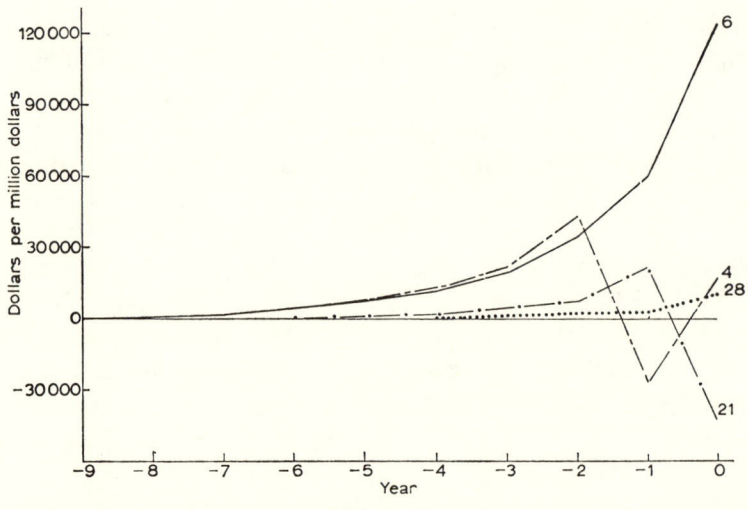

Figure 1

Elements of the dynamic inverse showing the direct and indirect effects of a million dollars' increase in the final demand for the products of industry 3, machinery products, in year 0 on the outputs of industries 4, 6, 21, 28 in this and the preceding years. —·—·—: transportation equipment and consumer appliances (4); ————: metals (6); ·—·—·—: lumber and products, excluding containers (21); ·······: rubber and plastic products (28).

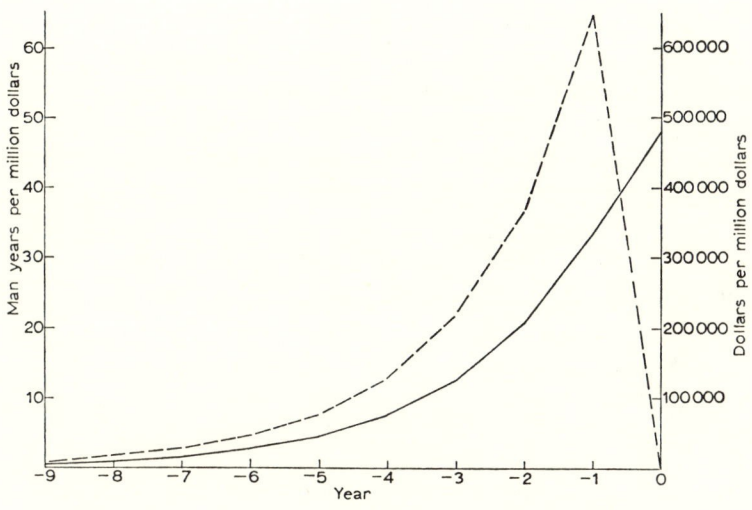

Figure 2

Time series of total direct and indirect labor and capital inputs required to deliver one million dollars' worth of the products of industry 3, machinery products, to final demand in year 0 (the left scale refers to labor, the right scale to capital). —————————: labor; ------------: capital.

estimated replacement requirements for consumers' durables. The rest of the latter is charged to a special household investment account, controlled by an appropriate vector of capital coefficients.

Labor requirements were computed on the basis of sectoral labor input coefficients, and total capital requirements for each sector were determined through summation of all elements of the appropriate column of the B matrix.

All inputs and outputs were measured both for 1947 and 1958 in 1958 prices. In other words, the units in terms of which the numerical computations were performed and their results presented should be interpreted as amounts of the respective commodities and services purchasable for one dollar at 1958 prices.

The entire computation absorbed about an hour's time on the IBM 7094 computer. The program included automatic plotting of the resulting time series by the machine. A selection of such plots is presented in the eight figures that I will now discuss.

Figure 1 illustrates the typical variety of shapes encountered among the time series, each of which constitutes a single element of

57

the dynamic inverse. Each of the four curves represents the time-phased amount of the product of one of the four different industries that were contributing directly or indirectly to supplying (in year 0) final users with one additional unit of the output of the machinery industry. Two of the inputs—"metals," and "rubber and plastic products"—are primary materials; their input curves ascend gradually but steadily from the beginning to the end. The demand for primary metals is much larger and anticipates the final delivery in significant amounts by some eight years. The first significant demand for rubber and plastic products is registered in the year −3.

The corresponding input requirements for transportation equipment and lumber, on the other hand, show a dip below the zero line in the years preceding the delivery of the final product. As explained above, this is typical of goods playing an important part in the process of capital accumulation.

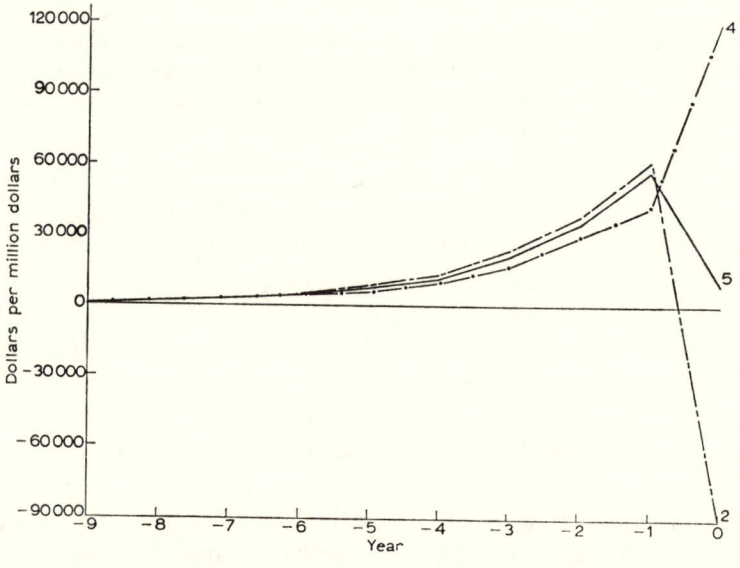

Figure 3

Elements of the dynamic inverse showing the alternative direct and indirect effects on the output of industry 6, metals, of a million dollars' worth of deliveries to final demand for the products of industries 2,4,5 in year 0. · — · —: transportation equipment and consumer appliances (4); — · — · —: textiles, clothing, furnishings (2); ————: construction (5).

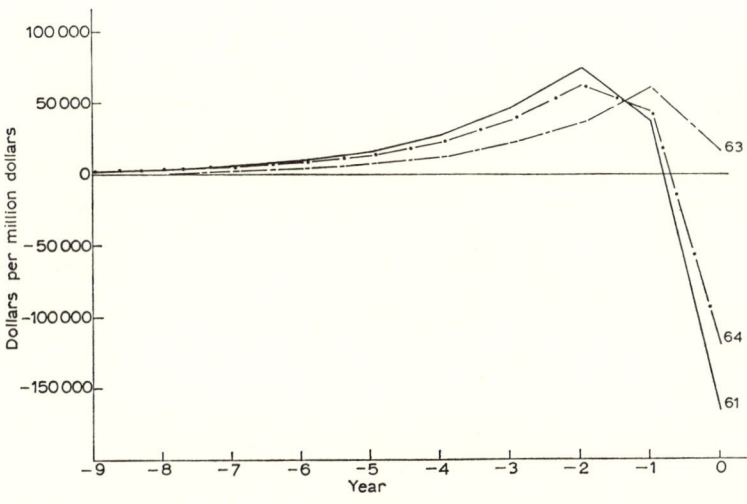

Figure 4

Elements of the dynamic inverse showing the alternative direct and indirect effects on the output of industry 6, metals, of a million dollars' worth of increases in the household, government, and total final demand in year 0. ————: household final demand (61); — · — · —: government final demand (63); · — · — · —: total final demand (64).

Figure 2 supplements Figure 1 by showing the amounts of labor and of capital, i.e., of investment goods, absorbed by *all industries* in the process of filling the direct and indirect input requirements for the delivery to final users (in year 0) of one million dollars' worth of the product of the machinery industry. The smoothness of the gradual rise is, of course, in both instances due to the mutual cancellation of irregularities in the employment and investment requirements of the many different individual industries combined in each of these two totals. The one year time-lag between the installation of new capacities and the delivery of additional outputs explains the last year's drop in the investment curve.

The differences among the reactions of the same industry to various kinds of final deliveries are shown in Figure 3. Metals behave as a typical raw material in their contribution to the production of transportation equipment—that is, mainly automobiles—delivered to final users; they react, however, as a typical investment good, in

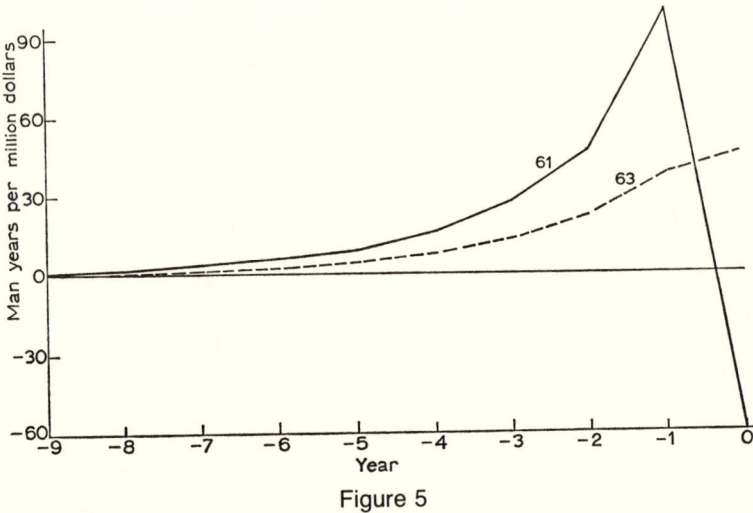

Figure 5

Time series of alternative direct and indirect labor inputs required to deliver a million dollars' worth of increases in the government and household final demand vectors in year 0. —————: household final demand (61); ------------: government final demand (63).

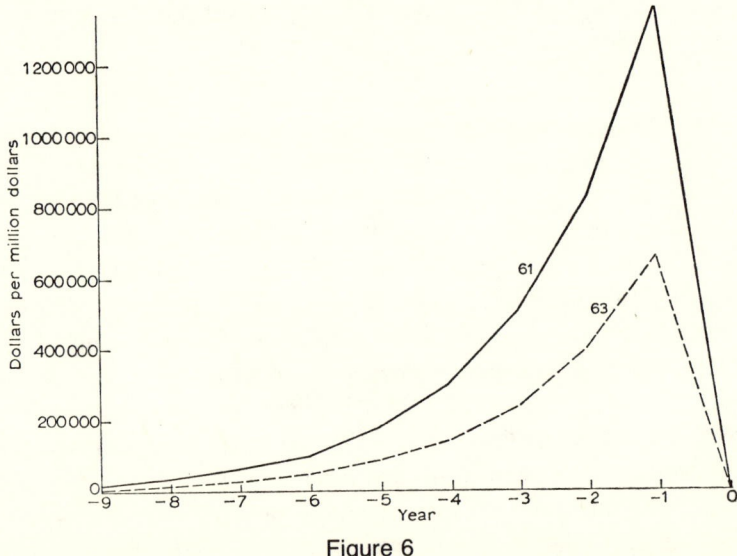

Figure 6

Time series of alternative direct and indirect capital inputs required to deliver a million dollars' worth of increases in the government and household final demand vectors in year 0.—————: household final demand (61); ------------: governmental final demand (63).

60

response to an increase in the final demand for textiles. An intermediate pattern of behavior marks the contribution of the metals sector to the satisfaction of the final demand for the output of the construction industry.

A similar difference can be seen in Figure 4 between the shapes of two time series, both tracing the requirements for products of the metal sector, one reflecting an additional million dollars' worth of government demand, the other anticipating a delivery of one million dollars' worth of goods and services demanded by households. The first curve reaches its crest one year before the final delivery can actually be made and stays above the zero line in the last; the second starts to fall off a year earlier and plunges below the zero line at the end. As should have been expected, the intermediate product mixture of the combined total demand yields an intermediate time profile weighted in favor of households.

The time series of total labor inputs contributing to the two principal components of final demand, as shown in Figure 5, are similar in shape to those shown in Figure 4. The same is true of the corresponding total capital requirements shown in Figure 6.

The three sets of curves in Figure 7 demonstrate how the dynamic inverse can reveal the effects of specified technical change on the dynamic properties of a given economic system. Each part of the chart presents the same element of the dynamic inverse in three alternative versions.

All three curves at the top represent the time-phased increase in the output of chemicals contributing directly and indirectly to the delivery of one additional million dollars' worth of food and drug products to final demand in the year 0. The first is computed on the basis of A_{1947} and B_{1947}, i.e., of the flow and capital coefficients characterizing the input structures of the 52 producing sectors of the American economy of the year 1947, the second on the basis of A_{1958} and B_{1958}, i.e., of 1958 technology. The third inverse was computed—in accordance with equation (4)—from a sequence of eleven different pairs of dated A and B matrices tracing the gradual shift from the 1947 to the 1958 technology. On the left this curve coincides with the first, but in the terminal year it catches up with the second.

The three sets of curves demonstrate how differently the same overall change can affect various elements of the same dynamic

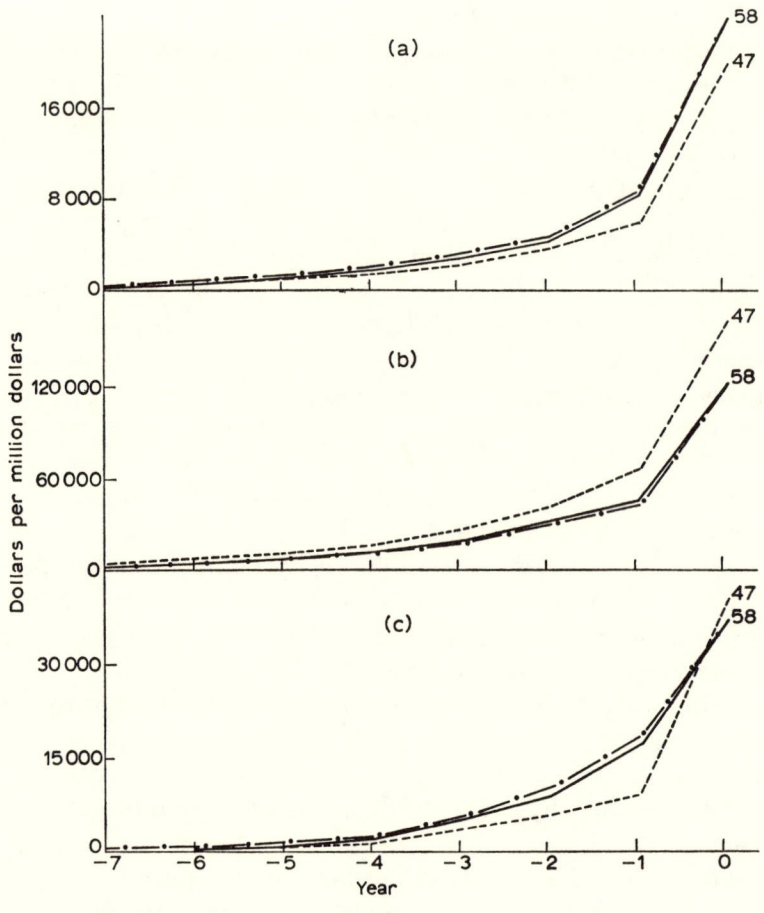

Figure 7

Effects of technological change on the elements of the dynamic inverse. (a) Time series of direct and indirect requirements for chemicals (8) to deliver a million dollars' worth of food and drugs (1) in year 0, computed on the basis of flow and capital coefficients representing the technologies of: ------------: 1947; · — · —: 1958; ———: shifting, year by year, from 1947 to 1958. (b) Time series of direct and indirect requirements for metals (6) to deliver a million dollars' worth of transportation equipment (4) in year 0, computed on the basis of flow and capital coefficients representing the technologies of: ----------: 1947; · — · —: 1958; ———: shifting, year by year, from 1947 to 1958. (c) Time series of direct and indirect requirements for chemicals (8) to deliver a million dollars' worth of nonferrous mining products (16) in year 0, computed on the basis of flow and capital coefficients representing the technologies of: ------------: 1947; · — · —: 1958; ———: shifting, year by year, from 1947 to 1958.

62

inverse. The combined effects of the many technical shifts reflected in the difference between the magnitude of the flow and the capital coefficients describing the input structures of the 52 sectors of the American economy in 1947 and 1958 led to an upward shift in the time series of chemical inputs required for delivery to final users of one million dollars' worth of food and drugs. The three curves in the middle part of the chart indicate that the same combination of structural changes reduced the inputs of metals contributing to the final delivery of consumers' appliances.

The contribution of chemicals to nonferrous metals mining shown on the bottom was affected by the same structural shifts in a more complicated way: The input requirements dropped in the last year of the series, i.e., the year of the final delivery, but they rose in all the previous years.

VI

The dynamic input-output system described above—not unlike the static input-output system—can be of little help in derivation of the golden rules of economic growth or in formulation of any other purely theoretical generalizations. It is too loosely jointed, too flexible for serving such an ambitious purpose. The dynamic inverse is primarily a storehouse of systematically organized factual information. This information is presented in a form particularly suitable for analytical description of intertemporal relations. The individual elements of the inverse can be spun into longer strands, each attached to a given time sequence of final deliveries. These strands can be woven into a broad fabric of intersectoral and intertemporal relationships which make up the analytical picture of economic growth.

Figure 8 illustrates graphically the structure of one such simple strand describing—or explaining, if you will—the increase in the level of output of primary metals called for by a delivery to final users of one million dollars' worth of nondurable consumers' goods (and of proportionally increased services of durable consumers' goods) per year over a period of 17 years. The first delivery to final users is made in the year 0, the last in the year +16.

Each of the partly superimposed curves represents the sequence of

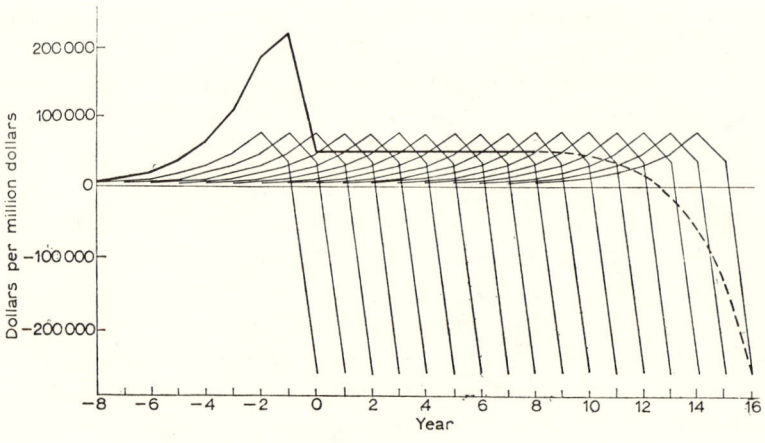

Figure 8

Direct and indirect effects on the output of industry 6, metals, of annual increases of a million dollars, continued over a 17-year period (years 0 through +16), in the household final demand vector (61).--------: effects of an increase in demand for a single year; ———: combined effects of all increases in annual demands.

inputs required for delivery of an additional million dollars' worth of consumers' goods to households. The year of final delivery is indicated by the position of the forward end of the curve. While the first delivery is due in the year 0, the first incremental input of nonnegligible size must be made in year −8. From then on, a new input sequence has to be started every year over a period of 17 years; the entire series of required total annual inputs—traced by the heavy black line on the chart—spans an interval of 25 years. The typical hump at the beginning reflects the buildup of the required additional capital stocks; the falling off at the end indicates, on the other hand, a reduction of these stocks, a gradual liquidation that sets in many years before the last delivery to households of an additional million dollars' worth of consumers' goods.

The flat portion of the curve marks what might be called the period of stationary reproduction, during which only current annual input requirements, including capital replacements, have to be covered. With the A and B matrices invariant and the vector of final deliveries, c, constant over a sufficiently long period of time, the corresponding

64

time-phased output vector, x, can—according to (5)—be determined as follows:

$$(6) \qquad x = (1 + R + R^2 + \cdots + R^m)\, G^{-1}c$$

If the series on the right-hand side converges,

$$x \to (1-R)^{-1}G^{-1}c = [G(1 - G^{-1}B)]^{-1}c = (G-B)^{-1}c = (1-A)^{-1}c$$

as $m \to \infty$.

Under stationary conditions governing the flat portion of the cumulative curve in Figure 8, the dependence of sectoral outputs on final demand is controlled by the static inverse, $(1-A)^{-1}$.

Information anticipating the level of final demand eight years hence would, in this particular case, suffice for a reasonably accurate assessment of direct and indirect input needs. The degree of foresight required depends, of course, on the profile of the elements of the inverse from which the total input curve has to be built up. So long as the total final demand continues to rise from year to year, no liquidation of productive stock is likely to be called for. In the summation of the overlapping series of direct and indirect effects of successive changes in final deliveries, the positive elements of the dynamic inverse will tend to dominate its few negative components.

In recent contributions to the pure theory of economic growth the problem of so-called terminal conditions has attracted much attention. According to the evidence presented above, the time horizon on which we could base our plans or make our projections should vary from sector to sector. The time shape of the elements of the dynamic inverse that governs direct and indirect requirements for the products of one particular industry might be such that its output in a given year depends primarily on the composition and the level of the final demand vector of the same year. For another industry that shape might be such that the level of its output in a given year reflects final deliveries, say, four or five years later.

VII

The balance equation (1), and consequently also the formulas describing the dynamic inverse derived from it, are based on the assumption of a uniform one-period ("one year") time lag between the installation of additional stocks of capital goods and the increase in the flow of output resulting from their first use. The same time unit enters into the definition of all the elements of the capital coefficient matrix B ("stocks per unit of *annual* output"). In fact, the time lags between the installation and initial full utilization of incremental capacities in various productive sectors of the U.S. economy—defined in terms of the degree of aggregation used in this study—seem to be around one year or somewhat shorter.

A change in the absolute magnitude of the time unit used in describing an actual economic system in terms of equations (1) would signify a corresponding real change in the length of all the lags. If, despite that change, the real capital requirements of all the sectors remain the same, the capital coefficients described by matrix B have to be "translated" into the new time unit. Thus, if the time lag is reduced from one year to half a year, all elements of B have to be multiplied by 2.

The effects of such a shift on the dominant characteristic root of the system and, consequently, on its convergence are analyzed in appendix I; changes in the time lags and in the magnitudes of the B coefficients tend to offset each other. The three curves entered in Figure 9 show how the time sequence of labor inputs required to increase total deliveries to final demand by one million dollars is affected if the basic structural investment lag is cut from one year to six or to four months. The horizontal axis of the graph is in natural years.

VIII

In static input-output analysis, the inverse of the structural matrix of a particular economy postmultiplied by a given column vector of final demand yields the vector of corresponding total sectoral outputs. The transpose of the same inverse when postmultiplied by a given vector of values added (wage, profit, tax, and other final payments disbursed by each industry per unit of its total physical output) yields the corresponding vector of equilibrium prices, i.e., of prices at which the total outlay (including the values added) of each sector would equal its aggregate receipts. In dynamic input-output analysis the transpose of the dynamic inverse determines the relationship between the time-phased vectors of values added in each of the producing sectors and the set of equilibrium prices that would balance the total outlays and the total receipts of each producing sector over time.

Let p_t represent a column vector, $_tp_1, _tp_2, \ldots, _tp_n$, of the prices of goods and services sold and purchased by various sectors in year t and v_t a column vector, $_tv_1, _tv_2, \ldots, _tv_n$, of the values added in each sector per unit of its output in year t. Value added can be best defined residually as all current outlays of a producing sector other than payments for inputs purchased from the same or from other industries.

Equation (7) below states that in any year t the prices of all goods represented by the vector on the left-hand side must equal their unit costs as represented by the terms appearing on the right-hand side. The product of the transpose of the flow coefficient matrix A' and the price vector p_t represents the costs of current inputs purchased by each productive sector from itself and from other industries. The elements of the value added (column) vector v_t comprise wages, rents, taxes, and profits paid out or charged per unit of its output by the respective industries in year t.

The two terms enclosed in the square brackets describe the unit

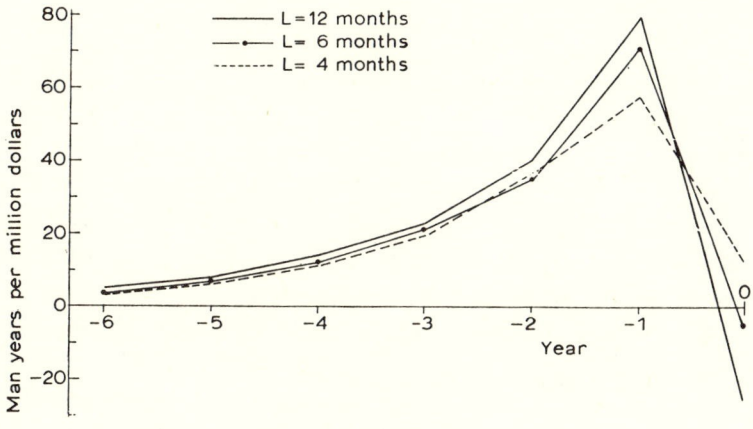

Figure 9

Direct and indirect labor inputs required to deliver an additional one million dollars' worth of goods to total final demand in year 0, assuming investment lags of 12 months, 6 months, and 4 months.

cost or gains conventionally booked through the capital account. For purposes of proper cost accounting, the stocks of capital goods are assumed to be acquired by each sector, in accordance with technological requirements, one year before the delivery of the output they produce and then sold off together with that output; in fact the sale will, in most cases, be purely nominal since the sector disposing of the capital goods will repurchase them again and again. Both transactions, of course, are supposed to be made at prices prevailing in the time period during which they take place. The value of capital stock purchased in the year $t - 1$ is multiplied by $1 + r_{t-1}$; r_{t-1} represents the annual money rate of interest prevailing in that year. As has been observed before, the stocks of capital released from production of outputs delivered in year t are employed at once to produce goods that will be delivered in the following year $t + 1$. The A and B matrices on the right-hand side are dated to reflect the process of technical change.

$$(7) \qquad P_t = A_t' p_t + [(1 + r_{t-1}) B_t' p_{t-1} - B_{t+1}' p_t] + v_t.$$

Equation (7) can be rewritten as

$$(8) \qquad\qquad G_t' p_t - \alpha_{t-1} B_t' p_{t-1} = v_t$$

where

$$G_t' = (1 - A_t' + B_{t+1}') \text{ and } \alpha_t = 1 + r_t$$

Assigning the values $-m$, $-m + 1$, $-m + 2$, . . . , -2, -1, 0, to the time subscript t, we can construct a system of interlocked equations analogous to (3). The structural matrix on the left-hand side of that new system would resemble the transpose of the structural matrix appearing in (3) with the difference that each of the B_t's is multiplied by a corresponding scalar, α_{t-1}.

The solution of that system for the unknown price vector p_0 in terms of the value added vectors of the same and all the previous years v_0, v_{-1}, v_{-2}, . . . , and of the corresponding "force of interest" factors α_0, α_{-1}, α_{-2}, . . . , has the form:

$$
\begin{aligned}
p_0 = {}& (G_0^{-1})' v_0 + (R_{-1} G_0^{-1})' \alpha_{-1} v_{-1} + (R_{-2} R_{-1} G_0^{-1})' \alpha_{-2} \alpha_{-1} v_{-2} \\
(9) \quad & +, \ldots, + (R_{-m} \ldots R_{-2} R_{-1} G_0^{-1})' \alpha_{-m} \ldots \alpha_{-2} \alpha_{-1} v_{-m} \\
& + (R_{-m} \ldots R_{-2} R_{-1} G_0^{-1})' \alpha_{-m} \ldots \alpha_{-2} \alpha_{-1} B_{-m}' p_{-(m+1)}
\end{aligned}
$$

The bracketed matrix products on the right-hand side of the first line are identical with the elements of the last column of the dynamic inverse appearing on the right-hand side of (4). These coefficients, however, enter into (9) in their transposed form. Since the series R_{-1}, $R_{-2}R_{-1}$, $R_{-3}R_{-2}R_{-1}$, . . . , converges toward 0, the last term on the right-hand side—containing the price vector $p_{-(m+1)}$—can be disregarded provided that the sequence is extended back over a sufficient number of years.

The price vector of any given year has thus been shown to depend on the value added vectors of that and of all preceding years. This dependence is governed by the transpose of the same dynamic inverse that determines the dated sequence of input requirements generated in the corresponding physical system by a given time-phased bill of goods. For example, in the absence of technical change and on the assumption that both the rate of interest and the value added vectors remain constant over time, equation (9) is reduced to

$$(10) \quad p_0 \rightarrow [G^{-1}]' \; [1 + R'\alpha + (R')^2\alpha^2 + (R')^3 \alpha^3 \cdots (R')^t\alpha^t]v$$

as $t \rightarrow \infty$.

After t becomes sufficiently large, the ratio between two successive terms of the exponential series on the right-hand side tends to equal $\mu_1\alpha$, where μ_1 is the dominant characteristic root of R'. The series will converge and thus yield a finite price vector p only if $\mu_1\alpha < 1$ or, since $\alpha = 1 + r$, if

$$r < \frac{1 - \mu_1}{\mu_1}.$$

The conclusion that, under certain conditions, the characteristic root of the matrix of an open dynamic input-output system imposes an upper limit on the rate of interest has been presented many years ago by Michio Morishima.[3]

Figure 10 shows how the price of the bundle[4] of consumers' goods delivered to final users in 1958 depends on the annual values added per unit of the metal industry's output. The solid curve, based on the

[3]Michio Morishima, *Equilibrium, Stability, and Growth* (London: Oxford University Press, 1964).
[4]A "final demand bundle" consists of goods, weighted according to 1958 consumption patterns, costing $1 in 1958 prices.

unrealistic assumption that the rate of interest through the entire 11-year period was equal to 0 (i.e., $\alpha = 1$), is identical with the corresponding solid curve in Figure 4. The dip below the zero line in the last year reflects negative costs, i.e., the revenue that would have been secured from the liquidation of capital stock purchased in the previous year. The positive expenditure on capital goods reflected in the other points of the same curve will, in most cases, offset this negative amount.

The other two curves were drawn on the assumption that interest rates of 10 and 25 percent respectively prevailed over the entire interval. They show how a rise in the interest rate increases the dependence of present prices on past values added (and, consequently, also on past prices).

Much of what I have said should have a familiar ring. The "productive advances" of Francois Quesnay, the process of expanded reproduction of Karl Marx, and the "roundabout production" of Böhm-Bawerk all contain the basic theoretical notions incorporated in the

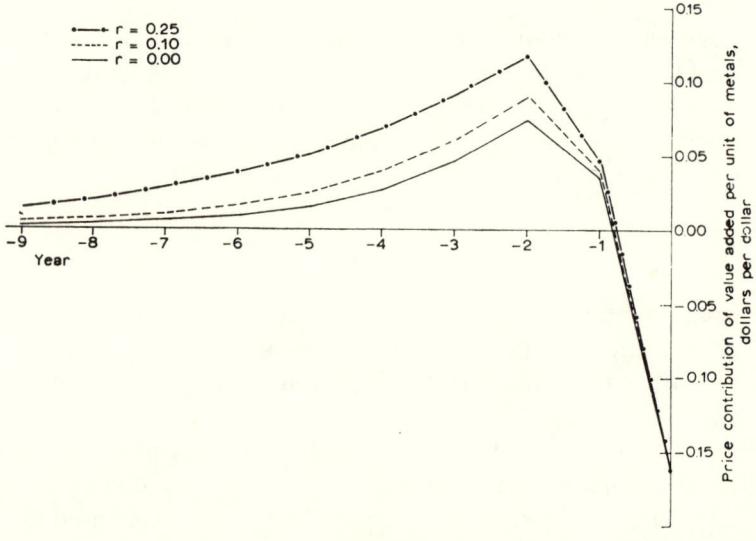

Figure 10

Portion of the price of a 1958 final demand bundle, directly and indirectly attributable to value added paid by the metal industry in year *t*.

derivation of the dynamic inverse. But while these great economists had to content themselves with verbal description and deductive reasoning, we can measure and we can compute. Therein lies the real difference between the past and the present state of economics.

Appendix I

To analyze the convergence properties of the series

$$(A1) \qquad R_{-1}, R_{-2}R_{-1}, R_{-3}R_{-2}R_{-1}, \ldots, R_{-t} \ldots R_{-3}R_{-2}R_{-1}$$
$$R_t = (1 - A_t + B_{t+1})^{-1} B_{t+1}$$

we can first consider the case in which,

$A_t = A$ and $B_t = B$, for all t's and consequently,
$R_t = R$ for all t's.

In this case, series (1) is transformed into the geometric series,

$$(A2) \qquad R, R^2, R^3, \ldots, R^t$$
$$(A3) \qquad R = (1 - A + B)^{-1}B$$
$$(A4) \qquad (1 - A + B) = (1 - A)[1 + (1 - A)^{-1}B]$$
$$(A5) \qquad (1 - A + B)^{-1}B = [1 + (1 - A)^{-1}B]^{-1}(1 - A)^{-1}B = (1 + U)^{-1}U$$

where $U = (1 - A)^{-1}B$.
Since $(1 - A)^{-1} > 0$, and $B \geqslant 0$ and is irreducible, therefore $U > 0$.

$$(A6) \qquad [(1 + U)^{-1}U]^{-1} = U^{-1}(1 + U) = (1 + U^{-1});$$

consequently

$$(A7) \qquad R = (1 + U^{-1})^{-1}.$$

Let λ_i $(i = 1, 2, 3, \ldots, n)$ represent the n roots of the square, nonsingular and indecomposable matrix U. Since $U > 0$, it has—according to the well-known theorem of Frobenius—a positive dominant simple root. Moreover, this root, and only this root, has associated with it a positive eigenvector. Let λ_1 be this root.

For real λ_i the corresponding roots of U^{-1} and of $1 + U^{-1}$ are, $1/\lambda_i$ and $1 + (1/\lambda_i)$, respectively. Thus according to equation (A7), the roots of R are

$$(A8) \qquad \mu_i = \frac{\lambda_i}{1 + \lambda_i} \text{ and in particular, } \mu_1 = \frac{\lambda_1}{1 + \lambda_1}.$$

From $\lambda_1 > 0$, it follows that $0 < \mu_1 < 1$, which means that R always has a simple positive root μ_1 smaller than 1, associated with a positive eigenvector.

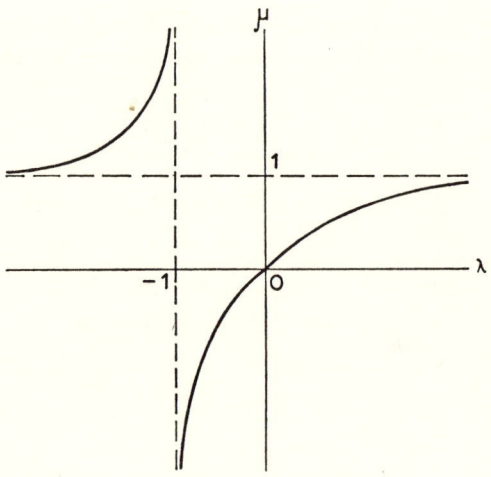

Figure A1

Schematic graph of relationship between μ and λ.

Figure A1 depicts the relationship between μ_i and λ_i for all real λ_i. If some of these subdominant roots are smaller than -0.5, the corresponding μ_i will be greater than 1 in absolute value. The eigenvectors associated with them will have elements of different signs.[5]

This implies that series R^1, R^2, R^3, . . . , could be divergent. Depending on whether the dominant root is real or complex and whether its real part is positive or negative, the elements of the corresponding dynamic inverse would, in this case, diverge—as one moves back in time—expanding without limit either monotonically in the positive or negative direction, or fluctuating with increasing amplitude between the positive and negative domain.

If R_t changes with t, but does so with infinite lower and upper limits, say, $\underline{R}$ and $\overline{R}$, its higher terms will lie between the corresponding higher terms of the series $\underline{R}^1$, $\underline{R}^2$, . . . , and $\overline{R}^1$, $\overline{R}^2$.

The convergence properties of the dynamic inverse depend on the time unit in terms of which the capital coefficients that enter into matrix B are defined. In the basic balance equation (1) that unit also represents the lag, i.e., the difference

[5]The analysis holds for complex roots with the following modification: Let $\lambda_i = a + b_i$.

Then, the real part of the corresponding μ_i becomes $\mathbf{R}(\mu_i) = \dfrac{a(a + 1) + b^2}{(a + 1)^2 + b^2}$.

To guarantee convergence, we must have $(a^2 + 1.5a) > -(b^2 + 0.5)$. If $b = 0$, these formulas reduce to the simpler form stated in the text.

between the time when additional stocks of capital goods, or inventories of current inputs, are accumulated and the time when they can be put to use.

Let t be a given time interval described in original units and t^* the same time interval measured in different units. If α is the ratio of the length of the first to that of the second unit,

$$(A9) \qquad\qquad t^* = \alpha t$$

If, for example, t describes a given stretch of time in years and t^* measures it in months, then, $\alpha = 12$.

The technical flow coefficients have no time dimensions; hence the elements of matrix A will remain the same after the time unit—and consequently the lag built into equation (A1)—has been changed from a year to, say, a month. But all the capital coefficients, that is, the elements of matrix B, will become 12 times larger. Continuing to use an asterisk to mark the values of matrices and their roots after the change of the time unit, we have

$$B^* = B\alpha$$
$$(A10) \qquad U^* = U\alpha \text{ and } 1 + U^{*-1} = 1 + U^{-1}/\alpha$$

It follows that,

$$\lambda_i^* = \lambda_i\alpha$$

and, in accordance with (A8)

$$(A11) \qquad\qquad \mu_i^* = \frac{\lambda_i/\alpha}{1 + \lambda_i/\alpha}$$

The relationship between μ_i^* and λ_i/α is thus the same as that between μ_i and λ_i explained above. Inspecting it we find that, if root μ_1 happens to be dominant, its dominance will not be affected by any change in the time unit and the lag. If, on the other hand, some other root μ_i were dominant and, consequently, the system were divergent, an increase in α, i.e., a shortening of the lag, if sufficiently large, could shift any negative magnitude λ_i/α into the interval between -0.5 and 0 and thus make μ_1^* dominant. A lengthening of the lag could, of course, have the opposite effect.

Appendix II

Concepts

I. A matrix
    The A matrix includes current flow coefficients and replacement coefficients. It is on a domestic output base.

II. *B* matrix

The *B* matrix is made up of the capital stock coefficients for all industries. Residential construction is included in the real estate and rental industry. The capital coefficients are capacity based.

III. Labor row

The labor row consists of "man-years" per thousand dollars of output.

IV. Total capital row

This row is simply the column sums of the *B* matrix.

V. Alternative bills of goods

A. Household nondurable goods including replacement of durable

This vector of final demand includes current purchases of nondurable goods and replacement of durable goods by households. It also contains a capital coefficient column, consisting of the stock of consumer durables (the stock of residential construction is in the real estate and rental column). The labor entry into this vector is domestic help.

B. Household goods, durable and nondurable

This vector of final demand contains current purchases of durable and nondurable goods by households.

C. Government

The government vector of final demand consists of purchases by the federal, state, and local governments.

D. Total final demand

Final demand includes expenditures by households (durable and nondurable goods), federal, state, and local governments, exports, and competitive imports. It excludes the gross private capital formation and net inventory change vectors.

All items are in 1958 prices.

1947 through 1958 data

Information regarding capital and technical coefficients is usually unavailable on a year-by-year basis. Since the dynamic model with technological change requires such data for, say, a dozen consecutive years, and since data may exist for no more than three years in this interval, most of the information has to be derived through interpolation. For most coefficients exponential interpolation is used to approximate a constant rate of growth. When one of the terminal year coefficients is zero, the exponential method becomes impractical, and the program approximates with a linear technique.

Suppose $a(47)$ and $a(58)$ represent corresponding elements of two terminal year matrices. Then,

if $a(47) > 0$ and $a(58) > 0$ exponential interpolation is used,
if $a(47) = 0$ and $a(58) > 0$ linear interpolation is used,
if $a(47) > 0$ and $a(58) = 0$ linear interpolation is used, and
if $a(47) = 0$ and $a(58) = 0$ linear interpolation is used.

Appendix III

Table A1—"59-order" classification

NUMBER	NAME	CORRESPONDING 83-ORDER SECTORS
1	Food and drugs	14, 15, 29
2	Textiles, clothing, furnishings	16, 17, 18, 19, 34, 22, 23
3	Machinery (just final)	51, 44, 45, 46, 47, 48, 49, 50, 63
4	Transportation equipment and consumer appliances	52, 54, 56, 59, 60, 61, 62
5	Construction	11, 12
6	Metals	37, 38
7	Energy	7, 31, 68
8	Chemicals	27
9	——	—
10	——	—
11	Livestock	1
12	Crops	2
13	Forestry	3
14	Agricultural services	4
15	Iron ore mining	5
16	Nonferrous ore mining	6
17	Petroleum mining	8
18	Stone and clay mining	9
19	Chemical mining	10
20	——	—
21	Lumber and products, excluding containers	20
22	Wooden containers	21
23	Paper products and containers	24, 25
24	——	—
25	Printing and publishing	26
26	Plastics and synthetics	28
27	Paint and allied products	30
28	Rubber and plastic products	32
29	Leather tanning	33
30	Glass and glass products	35
31	Stone and clay products	36
32	Metal containers	39
33	Heating, plumbing, structural metals	40
34	Stampings, screw machine products	41
35	Hardware, plating, valves, wire products	42
36	Engines and turbines	43
37	Electric apparatus and motors	53
38	Electric lighting and wiring equipment	55

NUMBER	NAME	CORRESPONDING 83-ORDER SECTORS
39	Electronic components	57
40	Batteries, X-ray and engine electrical equipment	58
41	Miscellaneous manufacturing	64
42	Transportation and warehousing	65
43	Communications, excluding radio and TV	66
44	Radio and TV broadcasting	67
45	Trade	69
46	Finance and insurance	70
47	Real estate and rental	71
48	Hotels, personal and repair services	72
49	Business services	73
50	Research and development	74
51	Automobile repair services	75
52	Amusements and recreation	76
53	Medical and educational institutions	77
54	——	—
55	——	—
56	Noncompetitive imports	80
57	Entertainment and business travel	81
58	——	—
59	Scrap and by-products	83
60	Total labor row	

Alternative bills of goods

{
61	Household nondurables including replacement of durables column	
62	Household durables and nondurables column	
63	Government final demand column	
64	Total final demand, excluding gross private capital formation and net inventory change, column	
65	Total capital row	
}

Appendix IV

Sources of data

1958 A matrix, current flow coefficients

This matrix is based on the 1958 input-output table published by the Office of Business Economics, Department of Commerce. See A.P. Carter, "Changes in the Structure of the American Economy, 1947 to 1958 and 1962," *Review of Economics and Statistics*, XLIX (May 1967).

1958 A matrix, replacement coefficients

This matrix was developed at the Harvard Economic Research Project based on 1958 capital coefficients and U.S. Treasury Department, Internal Revenue

Service, *Depreciation Guidelines and Rules*, Publication No. 456, U.S. Government Printing Office, Washington, D.C. (1964).

1958 *B* matrix, capital coefficients

The capital coefficients for manufacturing sectors were obtained from Waddell, Ritz, Norton, DeWitt, and Wood, *Capital Expansion Planning Factors, Manufacturing Industries*, National Planning Association, Washington, D.C. (April 1966). For nonmanufacturing sectors, the capital coefficients were compiled at the Harvard Economic Research Project by Samuel A. Rea, Jr., and others in 1966–1967.

1958 Labor coefficients

The labor coefficients are based on Jack Alterman, "Interindustry Employment Requirements," *Monthly Labor Review*, 88, No. 7 (July 1965).

1958 Final demand vectors

The final demand vectors are based on the 1958 input-output table published by the Office of Business Economics, Department of Commerce and on Raymond W. Goldsmith, *The National Wealth of the United States in the Postwar Period*, National Bureau of Economic Research, Princeton (1962).

1947 *A* matrix, current flow coefficients

This matrix is based on the Bureau of Labor Statistics 450-order input-output table for 1947, which was obtained by the Harvard Economic Research Project some years ago on cards (Deck A) from the Bureau of Labor Statistics along with mimeographed documentation for individual sectors. It is published at a 50-order level and is described in W. D. Evans and M. Hoffenberg, "The Interindustry Relations Study for 1947," *Review of Economics and Statistics*, XXXIV (May 1952). Adjustments have been made to the 1947 matrix in order to make it comparable with the 1958 matrix. See A. P. Carter, op. cit. Further work in this area is currently being done by Beatrice Vaccara and others at the Office of Business Economics and by the Harvard Economic Research Project.

1947 *A* matrix, replacement coefficients

This matrix was developed at the Harvard Economic Research Project, based on the 1947 capital coefficients and U.S. Treasury Department, op. cit.

1947 *B* matrix, capital coefficients

The 1947 capital coefficients are based on James M. Henderson and others, "Estimates of the Capital Structure of American Industries, 1947," mimeographed, Harvard Economic Research Project (June 1953), and Robert N. Grosse, *Capital Requirements for the Expansion of Industrial Capacity*, Vol. 1, Part 1, Executive Office of the President, Bureau of the Budget, Office of Statistical Standards (November 1953). Further revisions were made to the coefficients by Alan Strout and others in 1958–1962. Additional adjustments to make the 1947 capital coefficients comparable with the 1947 were made by Samuel A. Rea, Jr., and others (1966–1967) at the Harvard Economic Research Project.

1947 Labor coefficients

Same source as 1958 labor coefficients

1947 Final demand vectors

The final demand vectors are based on the Bureau of Labor Statistics 450-order input-output table and on Raymond W. Goldsmith, op. cit.

VI

Environmental repercussions and the economic structure: an input-output approach

I

Pollution is a by-product of regular economic activities. In each of its many forms it is related in a measurable way to some particular consumption or production process: The quantity of carbon monoxide released in the air bears, for example, a definite relationship to the amount of fuel burned by various types of automotive engines; the discharge of polluted water into our streams and lakes is linked directly to the level of output of the steel, the paper, the textile, and all the other water-using industries, and its amount depends, in each instance, on the technological characteristics of the particular industry.

Input-output analysis describes and explains the level of output of each sector of a given national economy in terms of its relationships to the corresponding levels of activities in all the other sectors. In its more complicated multiregional and dynamic versions the input-output approach permits us to explain the spatial distribution of output and consumption of various goods and services and of their growth or decline—as the case may be—over time.

This paper was presented in Tokyo, Japan, March 1970 at the International Symposium on Environmental Disruption in the Modern World held under the auspices of the International Social Science Council, Standing Committee on Environmental Disruption; published in *The Review of Economics and Statistics*, Vol. 52, No. 3, August 1970.

Peter Petri and Ed Wolff, both members of the research staff of the Harvard Economic Research Project, have programmed and carried out the computations described in this paper. For their invaluable assistance I owe my sincerest thanks.

Frequently unnoticed and too often disregarded, undesirable by-products (as well as certain valuable, but unpaid-for natural inputs) are linked directly to the network of physical relationships that govern the day-to-day operations of our economic system. The technical interdependence between the levels of desirable and undesirable outputs can be described in terms of structural coefficients similar to those used to trace the structural interdependence between all the regular branches of production and consumption. As a matter of fact, it can be described and analyzed as an integral part of that network.

It is the purpose of this report first to explain how such "externalities" can be incorporated into the conventional input-output picture of a national economy and, second, to demonstrate that—once this has been done—conventional input-output computations can yield concrete replies to some of the fundamental factual questions that should be asked and answered before a practical solution can be found to problems raised by the undesirable environmental effects of modern technology and uncontrolled economic growth.

II

Proceeding on the assumption that the basic conceptual framework of a static input-output analysis is familiar to the reader, I will link up the following exposition to the numerical examples and elementary equations presented in chapter 7 of my book entitled *Input-Output Economics* (New York: Oxford University Press, 1966).

Consider a simple economy consisting of two producing sectors, say, Agriculture and Manufacture, and Households. Each one of the two industries absorbs some of its annual output itself, supplies some to the other industry, and delivers the rest to final consumers—in this case represented by the Households. These intersectoral flows can be conveniently entered in an input-output table. See Table 1, for example. The magnitude of the total outputs of the two industries and of the two different kinds of inputs absorbed in each of them depends on, (1) the amounts of agricultural and manufactured goods that had to be delivered to the final consumers, i.e., the Households and, (2) the input requirements of the two industries determined by their specific technological structures. In this particular instance Agriculture is assumed to require 0.25 (= 25/100) units of agricultural and 0.14 (=

Table 1—Input-output table of a national
economy (in physical units)

INTO FROM	SECTOR 1 AGRICULTURE	SECTOR 2 MANUFACTURE	FINAL DEMAND HOUSEHOLDS	TOTAL OUTPUT
Sector 1 Agriculture	25	20	55	100 bushels of wheat
Sector 2 Manufacture	14	6	30	50 yards of cloth

14/100) units of manufactured inputs to produce a bushel of wheat, while the manufacturing sector needs 0.40 (= 20/50) units of agricultural and 0.12 (= 6/50) units of manufactured product to make a yard of cloth.

The "cooking recipes" of the two producing sectors can also be presented in a compact tabular form (see Table 2). This is the "structural matrix" of the economy. The numbers entered in the first column are the technical input coefficients of the Agriculture sector and those shown in the second are the input coefficients of the Manufacture sector.

III

The technical coefficients determine how large the total annual outputs of agricultural and of manufactured goods must be if they are to satisfy not only the given direct demand (for each of the two kinds of goods) by the final users, i.e., the Households, but also the intermediate demand depending in its turn on the total level of output in each of the two productive sectors.

These somewhat circular relationships are described concisely by the following two equations:

$$X_1 - 0.25X_1 - 0.40X_2 = Y_1$$
$$X_2 - 0.12X_2 - 0.14X_1 = Y_2$$

or in a rearranged form,

(1)
$$0.75X_1 - 0.40X_2 = Y_1$$
$$-0.14X_1 + 0.88X_2 = Y_2$$

X_1 and X_2 represent the unknown total outputs of agricultural and manufactured commodities respectively; Y_1 and Y_2 the given amounts of agricultural and manufactured products to be delivered to the final consumers.

These two linear equations with two unknowns can obviously be solved, for X_1 and X_2 in terms of any given Y_1 and Y_2.

Their "general" solution can be written in the form of the following two equations:

$$(2) \qquad \begin{aligned} X_1 &= 1.457Y_1 + 0.662Y_2 \\ X_2 &= 0.232Y_1 + 1.242Y_2. \end{aligned}$$

By inserting on the right-hand side the given magnitudes of Y_1 and Y_2 we can compute the magnitudes of X_1 and X_2. In the particular case described in Table 1, $Y_1 = 55$ and $Y_2 = 30$. Performing the necessary multiplications and additions one finds the corresponding magnitudes of X_1 and X_2 to be, indeed, equal to the total outputs of agricultural (100 bushels) and manufactured (50 yards) goods, as shown in Table 1.

The matrix, i.e., the square set table of numbers appearing on the right-hand side of (2),

$$(3) \qquad \begin{bmatrix} 1.457 & 0.662 \\ 0.232 & 1.242 \end{bmatrix}$$

is called the "inverse" of matrix,

$$(4) \qquad \begin{bmatrix} 0.75 & -0.40 \\ -0.14 & 0.88 \end{bmatrix}$$

describing the set constants appearing on the left-hand side of the original equations in (1).

Table 2—Input requirements per unit of output

INTO FROM	SECTOR 1 AGRICULTURE	SECTOR 2 MANUFACTURE
Sector 1 Agriculture	0.25	0.40
Sector 2 Manufacture	0.14	0.12

Any change in the technology of either Manufacture or Agriculture, i.e., in any one of the four input coefficients entered in Table 2, would entail a corresponding change in the structural matrix (4) and, consequently, in its inverse (3). Even if the final demand for agricultural (Y_1) and manufactured (Y_2) goods remained the same, their total outputs, X_1 and X_2, would have to change, if the balance between the total outputs and inputs of both kinds of goods were to be maintained. On the other hand, if the level of the final demands Y_1 and Y_2 had changed, but the technology remained the same, the corresponding changes in the total outputs X_1 and X_2 could be determined from the same general solution (2).

In dealing with real economic problems one, of course, takes into account simultaneously the effect both of technological changes and of anticipated shifts in the levels of final deliveries. The structural matrices used in such computations contain not two but several hundred sectors, but the analytical approach remains the same. In order to keep the following verbal argument and the numerical examples illustrating it quite simple, pollution produced directly by Households and other final users is not considered in it. A concise description of the way in which pollution generated by the final demand sectors can be introduced—along with pollution originating in the producing sectors—into the quantitative description and numerical solution of the input-output system is relegated to the Mathematical Appendix.

IV

As has been said before, pollution and other undesirable—or desirable—external effects of productive or consumptive activities should for all practical purposes be considered part of the economic system.

The quantitative dependence of each kind of external output (or input) on the level of one or more conventional economic activities to which it is known to be related must be described by an appropriate technical coefficient and all these coefficients have to be incorporated in the structural matrix of the economy in question.

Let it be assumed, for example, that the technology employed by the Manufacture sector leads to a release into the air of 0.20 grams of a solid pollutant per yard of cloth produced by it, while agricultural technology adds 0.50 grams per unit (i.e., each bushel of wheat) of its total output.

Using $\bar{X}_3$ to represent the yet unknown total quantity of this external output, we can add to the two original equations of output system (1) a third,

$$
\begin{aligned}
0.75X_1 - 0.40X_2 &= Y_1 \\
-0.14X_1 + 0.88X_2 &= Y_2 \\
0.50X_1 + 0.20X_2 - \bar{X}_3 &= 0
\end{aligned}
\tag{5}
$$

In the last equation the first term describes the amount of pollution produced by Agriculture as depending on that sector's total output, X_1, while the second represents, in the same way, the pollution originating in Manufacture as a function of X_2; the equation as a whole simply states that $\bar{X}_3$, i.e., the total amount of that particular type pollution generated by the economic system as a whole, equals the sum total of the amounts produced by all its separate sectors.

Given the final demands Y_1 and Y_2 for agricultural .and manufactured products, this set of three equations can be solved not only for their total outputs X_1 and X_2 but also for the unknown total output $\bar{X}_3$ of the undesirable pollutant.

The coefficients of the left-hand side of augmented input-output system (5) form the matrix,

$$
\tag{5a}
\left\{
\begin{array}{ccc}
0.75 & -0.40 & 0 \\
-0.14 & 0.88 & 0 \\
0.50 & 0.20 & -1
\end{array}
\right\}
$$

A "general solution" of system (5) would in its form be similar to the general solution (2) of system (1); only it would consist of three rather than two equations and the "inverse" of the structural matrix (4) appearing on the right-hand side would have three rows and columns.

Instead of inverting the enlarged structural matrix one can obtain the same result in two steps. First, use the inverse (4) of the original smaller matrix to derive, from the two-equation system (2), the outputs of agricultural (X_1) and manufactured (X_2) goods required to satisfy any given combination of final demands Y_1 and Y_2. Second, determine the corresponding "output" of pollutants, i.e., $\bar{X}_3$, by entering the values of X_1 and X_2 thus obtained in the last equation of set (5).

Let $Y_1 = 55$ and $Y_2 = 30$; these are the levels of the final demand for agricultural and manufactured products as shown on the input-output

Table 1. Inserting these numbers on the right-hand side of (5), we find—using the general solution (2) of the first two equations—that $X_1 = 100$ and $X_2 = 50$. As should have been expected they are identical with the corresponding total output figures in Table 1. Using the third equation in (5) we find, $X_3 = 60$. This is the total amount of the pollutant generated by both industries.

By performing a similar computation for $Y_1 = 55$ and $Y_2 = 0$ and then for $Y_1 = 0$ and $Y_2 = 30$, we could find out that 42.62 of these 60 grams of pollution are associated with agricultural and manufactured activities contributing directly and indirectly to the delivery to Households of 55 bushels of wheat, while the remaining 17.38 grams can be imputed to productive activities contributing directly and indirectly to final delivery of the 30 yards of cloth.

Had the final demand for cloth fallen from 30 yards to 15, the amount of pollution traceable in it would be reduced from 17.38 to 8.69 grams.

V

Before proceeding with further analytical exploration, it seems to be appropriate to introduce in Table 3 the pollution-flows explicitly in the original Table 1.

The entry at the bottom of the final column in Table 3 indicates that Agriculture produced 50 grams of pollutant and 0.50 grams per bushel of wheat. Multiplying the pollutant-output-coefficient of the manufacturing sector with its total output we find that it has contributed 10 to the grand total of 60 grams of pollution.

Table 3—Input-output table of the national economy with pollutants included (in physical units)

FROM \ INTO	SECTOR 1 AGRICULTURE	SECTOR 2 MANUFACTURE	HOUSEHOLDS	TOTAL OUTPUT
Sector 1 Agriculture	25	20	55	100 bushels of wheat
Sector 2 Manufacture	14	6	30	50 yards of cloth
Sector 3 Air pollution	50	10		60 grams of pollutant

INTO FROM	SECTOR 1 AGRICULTURE	SECTOR 2 MANUFACTURE	HOUSEHOLDS	TOTAL OUTPUT
Sector 1 Agriculture	25	20	55	100 bushels of wheat
Sector 2 Manufacture	14	6	30	50 yards of cloth
Labor inputs (value added)	80 ($80)	180 ($180)		260 man-years ($260)

Conventional economic statistics concern themselves with production and consumption of goods and services that are supposed to have some positive market value in our competitive private enterprise economy. This explains why the production and consumption of DDT are, for example, entered in conventional input-output tables while the production and consumption of carbon monoxide generated by internal combustion engines are not. Since private and public bookkeeping, which constitutes the ultimate source of the most conventional economic statistics, does not concern itself with such "nonmarket" transactions, their magnitude has to be estimated indirectly through detailed analysis of the underlying technical relationships.

Problems of costing and of pricing are bound to arise, however, as soon as we go beyond explaining and measuring pollution toward doing something about it.

VI

A conventional national or regional input-output table contains a "value-added" row. It shows, in dollar figures, the wages, depreciation charges, profits, taxes, and other costs incurred by each producing sector in addition to payments for inputs purchased from other producing sectors. Most of that "value added" represents the cost of labor, capital, and other so-called primary factors of production, and depends on the physical amounts of such inputs and their prices. The wage bill of an industry equals, for example, the total number of man-years times the wage rate per man-year.

In Table 4 the original national input-output table is extended to include the labor input or total employment row.

FROM \ INTO	SECTOR 1 AGRICULTURE	SECTOR 2 MANUFACTURE
Sector 1 Agriculture	0.25	0.40
Sector 2 Manufacture	0.14	0.12
Primary input-labor in man-hours (at $1 per hour)	0.80 ($0.80)	3.60 ($3.60)

The "cooking recipes" as shown in Table 2 can be accordingly extended to include the labor input coefficients of both industries expressed in man-hours as well as in money units.

In section III it was shown how the general solution of the original input-output system (2) can be used to determine the total outputs of agricultural and manufactured products (X_1 and X_2) required to satisfy any given combination of deliveries of these goods (Y_1 and Y_2) to final Households. The corresponding total labor inputs can be derived by multiplying the appropriate labor coefficients (l_1 and l_2) with each sector's total output. The sum of both products yields the labor input L of the economy as a whole.

$$(6) \qquad L = l_1X_1 + l_2X_2.$$

Assuming a wage rate of $1 per hour we find (see Table 5) the payment for primary inputs per unit of the total output to be $0.80 in Agriculture and $3.60 in Manufacture. That implies that the prices of one bushel of wheat (p_1) and of a yard of cloth (p_2) must be just high enough to permit Agriculture to yield a "value added" of v_1 (= 0.80) and Manufacture v_2 (= 3.60) per unit of their respective outputs after having paid for all the other inputs specified by their respective "cooking recipes."

$$p_1 - 0.25p_1 - 0.14p_2 = v_1$$
$$p_2 - 0.12p_2 - 0.40p_1 = v_2$$

or in a rearranged form,

$$
\begin{aligned}
0.75p_1 - 0.14p_2 &= v_1 \\
-0.40p_1 + 0.88p_2 &= v_2
\end{aligned}
\tag{7}
$$

The "general solution" of these two equations permitting one to compute p_1 and p_2 from any given combination of values added, v_1 and v_2 is,

$$
\begin{aligned}
p_1 &= 1.457v_1 + 0.232v_2 \\
p_2 &= 0.662v_1 + 1.242v_2
\end{aligned}
\tag{8}
$$

With $v_1 = \$0.80$ and $v_2 = \$3.60$ we have, $p_1 = \$2.00$ and $p_2 = \$5.00$. Multiplying the physical quantities of wheat and cloth entered in the first and second rows of Table 4 with appropriate prices, we can transform it into a familiar input-output table in which all transactions are shown in dollars.

VII

Within the framework of the open input-output system described above any reduction or increase in the output level of pollutants can be traced either to changes in the final demand for specific goods and services, changes in the technical structure of one or more sectors of the economy, or some combination of the two.

The economist cannot devise new technology, but, as has been demonstrated above, he can explain or even anticipate the effect of any given technological change on the output of pollutants (as well as of all the other goods and services). He can determine the effects of such a change on sectoral, and, consequently, also the total demand for the "primary factor of production." With given "values-added" coefficients he can, moreover, estimate the effect of such a change on prices of various goods and services.

After the explanations given above, a single example should suffice to show how any of these questions can be formulated and answered in input-output terms.

Consider the simple two-sector economy whose original state and structure were described in Tables 3, 4, 5, and 6. Assume that a process has been introduced permitting elimination (or prevention) of pollution and that the input requirements of that process amount to two man-years of labor (or \$2.00 of value added) and 0.20 yards of

OUTPUT SECTORS INPUTS AND POLLUTANTS' OUTPUT	SECTOR 1 AGRICULTURE	SECTOR 2 MANUFACTURE	ELIMINATION OF POLLUTANT
Sector 1 Agriculture	0.25	0.40	0
Sector 2 Manufacture	0.14	0.12	0.20
Pollutant (output)	0.50	0.20	
Labor (value added)	0.80 ($0.80)	3.60 ($3.60)	2.00 ($2.00)

cloth per gram of pollutant prevented from being discharged—either by Agriculture or Manufacture—into the air.

Combined with the previously introduced sets of technical coefficients this additional information yields the following complex structural matrix of the national economy.

The input-output balance of the entire economy can be described by the following set of four equations:

$$0.75X_1 - 0.40X_2 = Y_1 \quad \text{(wheat)}$$
$$(9) \quad -0.14X_1 + 0.88X_2 - 0.20X_3 = Y_2 \quad \text{(cotton cloth)}$$
$$0.50X_1 + 0.20X_2 - X_3 = Y_3 \quad \text{(pollutant)}$$
$$-0.80X_1 - 3.60X_2 - 2.00X_3 + L = Y_4 \quad \text{(labor)}$$

Variables:

X_1 : total output of agricultural products
X_2 : total output of manufactured products
X_3 : total amount of eliminated pollutant
L : employment
Y_1 : final demand for agricultural products
Y_2 : final demand for manufactured products
Y_3 : total uneliminated amount of pollutant
Y_4 : total amount of labor employed by Household
and other "final demand" sectors[1]

[1] In all numerical examples presented in this paper Y_4 is assumed to be equal to zero.

Instead of describing complete elimination of all pollution, the third equation contains on its right-hand side Y_3, the amount of uneliminated pollutant. Unlike all other elements of the given vector of final deliveries it is not "demanded" but, rather, tolerated.[2]

The general solution of that system for the unknown X's in terms of any given set of Y's is written out in full below

$$
\begin{aligned}
X_1 &= 1.573Y_1 + 0.749Y_2 - 0.149Y_3 + 0.000Y_4 \quad \text{Agriculture} \\
(10) \quad X_2 &= 0.449Y_1 + 1.404Y_2 - 0.280Y_3 + 0.000Y_4 \quad \text{Manufacture} \\
X_3 &= 0.876Y_1 + 0.655Y_2 - 1.131Y_3 + 0.000Y_4 \quad \text{Pollutant} \\
L &= 4.628Y_1 + 6.965Y_2 - 3.393Y_3 + 1.000Y_4 \quad \text{Labor}
\end{aligned}
$$

The square set of coefficients (each multiplied with the appropriate Y) on the right-hand side of (10) is the inverse of the matrix of constants appearing on the left-hand side of (9). The inversion was, of course, performed on a computer.

The first equation shows that each additional bushel of agricultural product delivered to final consumers (i.e., Households) would require (directly and indirectly) an increase of the total output of the agricultural sector (X_1) by 1.573 bushels, while the final delivery of an additional yard of cloth would imply a rise of total agricultural outputs by 0.749 bushels

The next term in the same equation measures the (direct and indirect) relationship between the total output of agricultural products (X_1) and the "delivery" to final users of Y_3 grams of uneliminated pollutants.

The constant -0.149 associated with it in this final equation indicates that a reduction in the total amount of pollutant delivered to final consumers by one gram would require an increase of agricultural output by 0.149 bushels.

Tracing down the column of coefficients asssociated with Y_3 in the second, third, and fourth equations we can see what effect a reduction in the amount of pollutant delivered to the final users would have on the total output levels of all other industries. Manufacture would have to produce an additional 0.280 yards of cloth. Sector 3, the antipollution industry itself, would be required to eliminate 1.131 grams of pollutant to make possible the reduction of its final delivery by 1

[2] In (6) that describes a system that generates pollution, but does not contain any activity combating it, the variable X_3 stands for the total amount of uneliminated pollution that is in system (8) represented by Y_3.

gram, the reason for this being that economic activities required (directly and indirectly) for elimination of pollution do, in fact, generate some of it themselves.

The coefficients of the first two terms on the right-hand side of the third equation show how the level of operation of the antipollution industry (X_3) would have to vary with changes in the amounts of agricultural and manufactured goods purchased by final consumers, if the amount of uneliminated pollutant (Y_3) were kept constant. The last equation shows that the total, i.e., direct and indirect, labor input required to reduce Y_3 by 1 gram amounts to 3.393 man-years. This can be compared with 4.628 man-years required for delivery to the final users of an additional bushel of wheat and 6.965 man-years needed to let them have one more yard of cloth.

Starting with the assumption that Households, i.e., the final users, consume 55 bushels of wheat and 30 yards of cloth and also are ready to tolerate 30 grams of uneliminated pollution, the general solution (10) was used to determine the physical magnitudes of the intersectoral input-output flows shown in Table 7.

The entries in the third row show that the agricultural and manufactured sectors generate 63.93 (= 52.25 + 11.68) grams of pollution of which 33.93 are eliminated by antipollution industry and the remaining 30 are delivered to Households.

VIII

The dollar figures entered in parentheses are based on prices the derivation of which is explained below.

The original equation, system (7), describing the price-cost relationships within the agricultural and manufacturing sectors has now to be expanded through inclusion of a third equation stating that the price of "eliminating one gram of pollution" (i.e., p_3) should be just high enough to cover—after payment for inputs purchased from other industries has been met—the value added, v_3, i.e., the payments to labor and other primary factors employed directly by the antipollution industry.

$$
\begin{aligned}
p_1 - 0.25p_1 - 0.14p_2 &= v_1 \\
p_2 - 0.12p_2 - 0.40p_1 &= v_2 \\
p_3 \qquad\quad - 0.20p_2 &= v_3
\end{aligned}
$$

Table 7—Input-output table of the national economy (surplus pollution is eliminatedby the antipollution industry)

INPUTS AND POLLUTANTS' OUTPUT	OUTPUT SECTORS SECTOR 1 AGRICULTURE	SECTOR 2 MANUFACTURE	ANTIPOLLUTION	FINAL DELIVERIES TO HOUSEHOLDS	TOTALS
Sector 1 Agriculture (bushels)	26.12 ($52.24)	23.37 ($46.74)	0	55 ($110.00)	104.50 ($208.99)
Sector 2 Manufacture (yards)	14.63 ($73.15)	7.01 ($35.05)	6.79 ($33.94)	30 ($150.00)	58.43 ($292.13)
Pollutant (grams)	52.25	11.68	−33.93	30 ($101.80 paid for elimination of 33.93 grams of pollutant)	
Labor (man-years)	83.60 ($83.60)	210.34 ($210.34)	67.86 ($67.86)	0	361.80 ($361.80)
Column Totals	$208.99	$292.13	$101.80	$361.80	

p_1 = $2.00, p_2 = $5.00, p_3 = $3.00, p_l = $1.00 (wage rate).

or in rearranged form,

$$
\begin{aligned}
(11) \quad & 0.75p_1 - 0.14p_2 && = v_1 \\
& -0.40p_1 + 0.88p_2 && = v_2 \\
& \qquad\quad\ - 0.20p_2 + p_3 && = v_3.
\end{aligned}
$$

The general solution of these equations—analogous to (8)—is

$$
\begin{aligned}
(12) \quad & p_1 = 1.457v_1 + 0.232v_2 \\
& p_2 = 0.662v_1 + 1.242v_2 \\
& p_3 = 0.132v_1 + 0.248v_2 + v_3.
\end{aligned}
$$

Assuming as before, $v_1 = 0.80$, $v_2 = 3.60$, and $v_3 = 2.00$, we find,

$$
\begin{aligned}
p_1 &= \$2.00 \\
p_2 &= \$5.00 \\
p_3 &= \$3.00
\end{aligned}
$$

The price (= cost per unit) of eliminating pollution turns out to be $3.00 per gram. The prices of agricultural and manufactured products remain the same as they were before.

Putting corresponding dollar values on all the physical transactions shown in the input-output Table 7 we find that the labor employed by the three sectors adds up to $361.80. The wheat and cloth delivered to final consumers cost $260.00. The remaining $101.80 of the value added earned by the Households will just suffice to pay the price, i.e., to defray the costs of eliminating 33.93 of the total of 63.93 grams of pollution generated by the system. These payments could be made directly or they might be collected in the form of taxes imposed on the Households and used by the government to cover the costs of the privately or publicly operated antipollution industry.

The price system would be different, if through voluntary action or to obey a special law, each industry undertook to eliminate, at its own expense, all or at least some specified fraction of the pollution generated by it. The added costs would, of course, be included in the price of its marketable product.

Let, for example, the agricultural and manufacturing sectors bear the costs of eliminating, say, 50 percent of the pollution that, under prevailing technical conditions, would be generated by each one of them. They may either engage in antipollution operations on their own account or pay an appropriately prorated tax.

In either case the first two equations in (11) have to be modified by inclusion of additional terms: the outlay for eliminating 0.25 grams and 0.10 grams of pollutant per unit of agricultural and industrial output respectively.

$$
\begin{aligned}
0.75p_1 - 0.14p_2 - 0.25p_3 &= v_1 \\
-0.40p_1 + 0.88p_2 - 0.10p_3 &= v_2 \\
- 0.20p_2 + \quad p_3 &= v_3.
\end{aligned}
$$
(13)

The "inversion" of the modified matrix of structural coefficients appearing on the left-hand side yields the following general solution of the price system:

$$
\begin{aligned}
p_1 &= 1.511v_1 + 0.334v_2 + 0.411v_3 \\
p_2 &= 0.703v_1 + 1.318v_2 + 0.308v_3 \\
p_3 &= 0.141v_1 + 0.264v_2 + 1.062v_3.
\end{aligned}
$$
(14)

With "values added" in all the three sectors remaining the same as they were before (i.e., $v_1 = \$.80$, $v_2 = \$3.60$, $v_3 = \$2.60$) these new sets of prices are as follows:

$$
\begin{aligned}
p_1 &= \$3.234 \\
p_2 &= \$5.923 \\
p_3 &= \$3.185
\end{aligned}
$$

While purchasing a bushel of wheat or a yard of cloth the purchaser now pays for elimination of some of the pollution generated in production of that good. The prices are now higher than they were before. From the point of view of Households, i.e., of the final consumers, the relationship between real costs and real benefits remains, nevertheless, the same; having paid for some antipollution activities indirectly he will have to spend less on them directly.

IX

The final Table 8 shows the flows of goods and services between all the sectors of the national economy analyzed above. The structural characteristics of the system—presented in the form of a complete set of technical input-output coefficients—were assumed to be given; so was the vector of final demand, i.e., quantities of products of each industry delivered to Households (and other final users) as well as

Table 8—Input-output table of a national economy with pollution-related activities presented separately

| | AGRICULTURE | | | MANUFACTURE | | | | FINAL DELIVERIES TO HOUSEHOLDS | NATIONAL TOTALS |
	Wheat	Anti-pollution	Total	Cloth	Anti-pollution	Total	ANTI-POLLUTION		
Agriculture	26.12 ($84.47)	0	26.12 ($84.47)	23.37 ($75.58)	0	23.37 ($75.58)	0	55 ($177.87)	105.50 ($337.96)
Manufacture	14.63 ($86.65)	5.23 ($30.98)	19.86 ($117.63)	7.01 ($41.52)	1.17 ($6.93)	8.18 ($48.45)	.39 ($2.33)	30 ($177.69) 30	58.43 ($346.07)
Pollutant	52.25	−26.13	26.12	11.69	−5.85	5.84	−1.97	($6.26 paid for elimination of 1.97 grams of pollutant)	
Labor (value added)	83.60 ($83.60)	52.26 ($52.26)	135.86 ($135.86)	210.34 ($210.34)	($11.70) ($11.70)	($222.04) ($222.04)	($3.93) ($3.93)		361.80 ($361.80)
Total Costs	($254.72)	($83.24)	($337.96)	($327.44)	($18.63)	($346.07)	($6.26)	($361.80)	

$p_1 = \$3.23$, $p_2 = \$5.92$, $p_3 = \$3.19$.
$v_1 = \$0.80$, $v_2 = \$3.60$, $v_3 = \$2.00$.

the uneliminated amount of pollutant that, for one reason or another, they are prepared to "tolerate." Each industry is assumed to be responsible for elimination of 50 percent of the pollution that would have been generated in the absence of such countermeasures. The Households defray—directly or through tax contributions—the cost of reducing the net output of pollution still further to the amount that they do, in fact, accept.

On the basis of this structural information we can compute the outputs and the inputs of all sectors of the economy, including the antipollution industries, corresponding to any given "bill of final demand." With information on "value added," i.e., the income paid out by each sector per unit of its total output, we can, furthermore, determine the prices of all outputs, the total income received by the final consumer and the breakdown of their total expenditures by types of goods consumed.

The 30 grams of pollutant entered in the "bill of final demand" are delivered free of charge. The $6.26 entered in the same box represent the costs of that part of antipollution activities that were covered by Households directly, rather than through payment of higher prices for agricultural and manufactured goods.

The input requirements of antipollution activities paid for by the agricultural and manufacturing sectors and all the other input requirements are shown separately and then combined in the total input columns. The figures entered in the pollution row show accordingly the amount of pollution that would be generated by the principal production process, the amount eliminated (entered with a minus sign), and finally the amount actually released by the industry in question. The amount (1.97) eliminated by antipollution activities not controlled by other sectors is entered in a separate column that shows also the corresponding inputs.

From a purely formal point of view the only difference between Table 8 and Table 7 is that in the latter all input requirements of Agriculture and Manufacture and the amount of pollutant released by each of them are shown in a single column, while in the former the productive and antipollution activities are described also separately. If such subdivision proves to be impossible and if, furthermore, no separate antipollution industry can be identified, we have to rely on the still simpler analytical approach that led up to the construction of Table 3.

Once appropriate sets of technical input and output coefficients have been compiled, generation and elimination of all the various kinds of pollutants can be analyzed as what they actually are—integral parts of the economic process.

Studies of regional and multiregional systems, multisectoral projections of economic growth and, in particular, the effects of anticipated technological changes, as well as all other special types of input-output analysis can, thus, be extended so as to cover the production and elimination of pollution as well.

The compilation and organization of additional quantitative information required for such extension could be accelerated by systematic utilization of practical experience gained by public and private research organizations already actively engaged in compilation of various types of input-output tables.

Mathematical appendix

Static-open input-output system with pollution-related activities built in

Notation

Commodities and services

$1, 2, 3, \ldots i \ldots j \ldots m, m + 1, m + 2, \ldots g \ldots k \ldots n$
    useful goods   pollutants

Technical coefficients

a_{ij}—input of good i per unit of output of good j (produced by sector j)
a_{ig}—input of good i per unit of eliminated pollutant g (eliminated by sector g)
a_{gi}—output of pollutant g per unit of output of good i (produced by sector i)
a_{gk}—output of pollutant g per unit of eliminated pollutant k (eliminated by sector k)
r_{gi}, r_{gk}—proportion of pollutant g generated by industry i or k eliminated at the expense of that industry

Variables
x_i—total output of good i
x_g—total amount of pollutant g eliminated
y_i—final delivery of good i (to Households)
y_g—final delivery of pollutant g (to Households)
p_1—price of good
p_g—the "price" of eliminating one unit of pollutant g

v_i—"value added" in industry i per unit of good i produced by it
v_g—"value added" in antipollution sector g per unit of pollutant g eliminated by it

Vectors and matrices

$$A_{11} = [a_{ij}] \qquad i, j = 1, 2, 3, \ldots, m$$
$$A_{21} = [a_{gi}] \quad \left.\begin{array}{l} i = 1, 2, 3, \ldots, m \end{array}\right.$$
$$A_{12} = [a_{ig}] \quad \left.\begin{array}{l} g = m + 1, m + 2, m + 3, \ldots, n \end{array}\right.$$
$$A_{22} = [a_{gk}] \qquad g, k = m + 1, m + 2, m + 3, \ldots, n$$
$$Q_{21} = [q_{gi}] \qquad i = 1, 2, \ldots, m$$
$$\qquad\qquad\qquad g = m + 1, m + 2, \ldots, n$$
$$Q_{22} = [q_{gk}] \qquad g, k = m + 1, m + 2, \ldots, n$$

where $q_{gi} = r_{gi} a_{gi}$

$\qquad\quad q_{gk} = r_{gk} a_{gk}$

$$X_1 = \begin{Bmatrix} x_1 \\ x_2 \\ \cdot \\ \cdot \\ \cdot \\ x_m \end{Bmatrix} \qquad Y_1 = \begin{Bmatrix} y_1 \\ y_2 \\ \cdot \\ \cdot \\ \cdot \\ y_m \end{Bmatrix} \qquad V_1 = \begin{Bmatrix} v_1 \\ v_2 \\ \cdot \\ \cdot \\ \cdot \\ v_m \end{Bmatrix}$$

$$X_2 = \begin{Bmatrix} x_{m+1} \\ x_{m+2} \\ \cdot \\ \cdot \\ \cdot \\ x_n \end{Bmatrix} \qquad Y_2 = \begin{Bmatrix} y_{m+1} \\ y_{m+2} \\ \cdot \\ \cdot \\ \cdot \\ y_n \end{Bmatrix} \qquad V_2 = \begin{Bmatrix} v_{m+1} \\ v_{m+2} \\ \cdot \\ \cdot \\ \cdot \\ v_n \end{Bmatrix}$$

PHYSICAL INPUT-OUTPUT BALANCE

$$(15) \quad \begin{bmatrix} I - A_{11} & \vdots & -A_{12} \\ \cdots & \cdots & \cdots \\ A_{21} & \vdots & -I + A_{22} \end{bmatrix} \begin{bmatrix} X_1 \\ \cdots \\ X_2 \end{bmatrix} = \begin{bmatrix} Y_1 \\ \cdots \\ Y_2 \end{bmatrix}$$

$$(16) \quad \begin{bmatrix} X_1 \\ \cdots \\ X_2 \end{bmatrix} = \begin{bmatrix} I - A_{11} & \vdots & -A_{12} \\ \cdots & \cdots & \cdots \\ A_{21} & \vdots & -I + A_{22} \end{bmatrix}^{-1} \begin{bmatrix} Y_1 \\ \cdots \\ Y_2 \end{bmatrix}$$

INPUT-OUTPUT BALANCE BETWEEN PRICES AND VALUES ADDED

$$(17) \quad \begin{bmatrix} I - A'_{11} & \vdots & -Q'_{21} \\ \cdots & \cdots & \cdots \\ -A'_{12} & \vdots & I - Q'_{22} \end{bmatrix} \begin{bmatrix} P_1 \\ P_2 \end{bmatrix} = \begin{bmatrix} V_1 \\ V_2 \end{bmatrix}$$

$$(18) \quad \begin{bmatrix} P_1 \\ \cdots \\ P_2 \end{bmatrix} = \begin{bmatrix} I - A'_{11} & \vdots & -Q'_{21} \\ \cdots & \cdots & \cdots \\ -A'_{12} & \vdots & I - Q'_{22} \end{bmatrix}^{-1} \begin{bmatrix} V_1 \\ V_2 \end{bmatrix}$$

Supplementary notation and equations accounting for pollution generated directly by final consumption

Notation

Technical coefficients

$a_{gy, (i)}$—output of pollutant generated by consumption of one unit of commodity i delivered to final demand.

Variables

y_g^*—sum total of pollutant g "delivered" from all industries to and generated within the final demand sector,

x_g^*—total gross output of pollutant g generated by all industries and in the final demand sector.

$$A_y = \begin{Bmatrix} a_{m+1, \, y(1)} & a_{m+1, \, y(1)} & \cdots & a_{m+1, \, y(m)} \\ a_{m+2, \, y(2)} & a_{m+2, \, y(2)} & \cdots & a_{m+2, \, y(m)} \\ \cdot & \cdot & & \\ \cdot & \cdot & & \\ \cdot & \cdot & & \\ a_n \, y_1 & a_n \, y_2 & \cdots & a_n \, y_m \end{Bmatrix}$$

$$Y_2^* = \begin{Bmatrix} y^*_{m+1} \\ y^*_{m+2} \\ \cdot \\ \cdot \\ \cdot \\ y_n^* \end{Bmatrix} \qquad x_g^* = \begin{Bmatrix} x^*_{m+1} \\ x^*_{m+2} \\ \cdot \\ \cdot \\ \cdot \\ x_n^* \end{Bmatrix}$$

In case some pollution is generated within the final demand sector itself, the vector Y_2 appearing on the right-hand side of (15) and (16) has to be replaced by vector $Y_2 - Y_2^*$, where

$$(19) \qquad Y_2^* = A_y Y_1.$$

The price-value added equations (17), (18) do not have to be modified.

Total gross output of pollutants generated by all industries and the final demand sector does not enter explicitly in any of the equations presented above; it can, however, be computed on the basis of the following equation,

$$(20) \qquad X^* = [A_{21} \; \vdots \; A_{22}] \begin{bmatrix} X_1 \\ \cdots \\ X_2 \end{bmatrix} + Y_2^*.$$

VII

National income, economic structure, and environmental externalities

I. National income as a welfare index

The per capita net national income used as a measure of the level of welfare is a typical index number. The computation of an index number involves application of some well-defined but essentially arbitrary conventional procedures to direct or indirect measurements of observed, or at least in principle observable, phenomena.

The conventional interpretation of net national income valued in some constant prices can be conveniently rationalized in terms of the ad hoc assumption that preferences of a representative average consumer can be described by a social utility function or a fixed set of well-behaving social indifference curves.

At this point observed or at least observable facts come in. The bundle of goods actually consumed by a representative individual has been obviously preferred—so goes the argument—to all the other alternative bundles that were accessible to him.

Under the special conditions of a market economy the set of all alternative bundles accessible to a representative consumer is uniquely determined by (a) the amounts of various goods that he has actually consumed and (b) the relative prices of these goods. The relative prices represent the marginal opportunity costs of each good in terms of every other good as seen from the point of their actual or potential consumer.

From M. Moss (ed.), *The Measurement of Economic and Social Performance*, Studies in Income and Wealth, Vol. 38 (New York: National Bureau of Economic Research, 1973), pp. 565–76.

This factual information, combined with the before-mentioned ad hoc assumption concerning the existence of a "well-behaved" set of collective indifference lines, permits us to identify *some* of the bundles of goods that the representative consumer apparently judges to be *less desirable* than the particular bundle that he actually chose to use.

This analytical proposition constitutes the basic, not to say the sole, theoretical justification for interpreting the *differences* in per capita net national income—valued in fixed prices—as an index of changes in the level of average per capita welfare attained by a particular society in different years.

Goods acquired through other means than purchases at given prices on a free market can still be taken into account in computation of the conventional welfare index provided their opportunities costs—as perceived by the representative consumer—can be ascertained in some other way.

Much of the work aimed at inclusion of various nonmarketable components into the measure of national income is centered on devising plausible methods of determining the imputed prices or more generally the opportunity costs of such goods.

In the light of what has been said above, the inclusion of pollutants and other kinds of environmental repercussions of economic activities into the measurement of the per capita national income as a welfare index requires answers to two sets of questions. One concerns the establishment of acceptable conventions pertaining to the inclusion of environmental repercussions into the conceptual framework of an all-embracing social utility function and a corresponding set of representative indifference curves. The other pertains to the actual physical description and measurement of the generation and elimination of pollutants by the economic system and the empirical determination of their opportunity costs in terms of ordinary goods and of each other.

The answer that one can give to these questions is critically influenced by the typically external nature of most environmental repercussions of economic activities and also by the fact that because of that measures aimed at abatement of their undesirable effects must in most instances be promulgated by the government.

Speaking in this context of collective indifference lines or preferences of a representative individual one must interpret such preference—at least so far as the environmental effects of economic activities are concerned—as being revealed not through private but rather through collective choice reflected in specific actions of the government.

Moreover, in case the conjectured opportunity costs reflected in the level of antipollution actions actually observed differ from the true opportunity costs, it is the former rather than the latter that would have to provide the base for proper weighing of pollution components to be included in a revised, more comprehensive, national income index.

Who would pretend to know what opportunity costs (if any) are being taken into account in the design of antipollution measures now actually being carried out in the United States?

Many of the contributors to the present symposium when touching upon problems of social valuation abandon the difficult revealed preference criteria in favor of a strictly axiomatic approach.

That solves the problem of welfare measurement as simply as Columbus solved his problem with the egg. One chooses ad hoc a social utility function which for some ethical or mathematical reason is appealing, inserts into it the levels of consumption of ordinary goods and net output of pollutants as they actually are, and then compares the index of welfare thus attained with the highest number of points that could be reached if the society were to move to the optimal point along the empirically given opportunity costs frontier.

Who can decide, however, what social utility function one should finally choose? Certainly not the economists in their professional capacity!

II. Enlarged input-output table, structural coefficients, and intersectoral dependence

Exhibit 1 presents a schematic outline of an expanded input-output table that traces not only the intersectoral flows of ordinary commodities and services, but also the generation and elimination of pollutants. The conventional classification of economic activities and goods is accordingly expanded to include the names of various pollutants and activities aimed at their elimination.

(1,1) Inputs of (ordinary) goods into industries. Most of these goods are produced by industries listed on the left, but some might originate as the "by-product" in pollution-eliminating activities. See (1,3).

(1,2) Inputs of ordinary goods into various pollution-eliminating activities and outputs of ordinary goods (entered with a negative sign) generated as by-products of pollution-eliminating activities. Reprocessed materials, for example, are entered here.

(1,3A) Goods delivered to the final demand sector are entered along the main diagonal of this square. See (3,3B).

(1,4) These totals do not include amounts of ordinary goods (as their by-products) originating in the pollution-eliminating activities and thus represent the activity levels of ordinary industries.

(2,1) Each row shows the amounts of one particular pollutant generated by industries listed at the heads of different columns. In other words, pollutants are treated here the way by-products are treated in ordinary input-output tables.

(2,2) Along each row are entered—as negative numbers—the amounts of one particular pollutant eliminated by activities named at the heads of different columns. The amounts of a pollutant generated, as is often the case, in the process of elimination of some other pollutants are entered along its appropriate row as positive numbers.

(2,3A), (2,3B) For purely descriptive purposes the total amounts of various pollutants generated in the final demand sector can be presented in a single column. For purposes of structural analyses, however, these totals should be distributed among as many separate columns as there are different inputs, i.e., industrial product inputs and primary factor inputs, absorbed by the final demand sector. In the process of final consumption each of these inputs is liable to generate its own "column" of pollutants. The inputs of ordinary goods into the final demand sector are entered in rows along the main diagonal of the square formed by (1,2) and (2,2) considered together. It sounds rather complicated, but that is the price one has to pay for orderly bookkeeping.

Exhibit 1

Interindustrial flows expanded to include the generation and elimination of pollutants

	Industries 1	Pollution-eliminating Activities 2	Final Demand Sector 3		Totals 4
Industries 1	(1,1) Inputs of goods into industries (+) $[a_{ij}]$	(1,2) Inputs of goods into pollution eliminating activities (+) Output of goods by pollution eliminating activities (−) $[a_{ig}]$	(1,3A) Delivery of goods to final demand sector (+)	(1,3B) (Empty)	(1,4) Total outputs of goods excluding the amounts generated by the pollution eliminating activities
Pollutants 2	(2,1) Outputs of pollutants by industries (+) $[a_{gi}]$	(2,2) Elimination of pollutants by pollution eliminating activities (−) Output of pollutants by pollution eliminating activities (+) $[a_{gk}]$	(2,3A) Outputs of pollutants by final demand sector (connected with the consumption of goods) (+) $[c_{gi}]$	(2,3B) Outputs of pollutants by the final demand sector (connected with the consumption of primary factors) (+) $[c_{gf}]$	(2,4) *Net* outputs of pollutants (+)
Primary Inputs 3	(3,1) Inputs of primary factors into industries (+) $[v_{fi}]$	(3,2) Inputs of primary factors into pollution eliminating activities (+) $[v_{fg}]$	(3,3A) (Empty)	(3,3B) Delivery of primary factors to final demand sector (+)	(3,4) Total inputs of primary factors (+)

(2,4) Each figure in this column is obtained by subtracting the sum of all negative from the sum of all positive entries appearing to the left along the entire length of the row. These are the undesirable *net* outputs of various pollutants delivered by the economic system to the final users alongside the desirable ordinary goods and primary factors entered in (1,3A) and (3,3B). Together they make up the final results of economic activities upon which the welfare of the society supposedly depends.

(3,1), (3,2), (3,3B), (3,4) These contain a single row of aggregated value-added figures or several rows of physical or dollar figures depending on the amount of detail one wants to present.

The entries are organized in such a way as to have each column contain inputs and outputs controlled by the same autonomous set of structural relationships (i.e., by the same "cooking recipe"). The table is subdivided into rows and corresponding column strips. Each strip can be thought of as containing many rows of figures not shown in this schematic presentation. Each of the rectangular intersections on a row and a column can be conveniently identified by two numbers.

All entries can be interpreted as representing physical quantities measured in appropriate physical units or indices of physical amounts. All dollar figures appearing in the table can be interpreted as such indices (with a defined or undefined base). Hence, the usual *column* sums are pointedly omitted.

III. Structural relationships and opportunity costs

The figures entered in each one of the separate columns of the first three vertical strips of the enlarged flow table can be interpreted as representing the inputs absorbed and outputs generated by one particular process carried on side by side with many other structurally different processes within the framework of the given economic system.

Assuming that the structure of each such process can be described in terms of a linear or at least linearized "cooking recipe," the actual level of each output and each input as entered in the flow table can be interpreted as a product of two numbers: a technical coefficient and a number describing the level at which the process that absorbs that particular input or generates that particular output actually operates.

The levels of operation of ordinary industries are usually measured in terms of their principal output, while the level of operation of a pollution-eliminating activity can be conveniently described by the number of units of the specific pollutant that it eliminates. The levels of consumption activities that might generate pollution are described by the number of units of a particular good or primary factor delivered to the final demand sector.

The structural matrix of the economy—corresponding to the enlarged flow table described above—can be written in the following partitioned form:

	1	2	3 A	B
1	$[a_{ij}]$	$[a_{ig}]$		
2	$[a_{gi}]$	$[a_{gk}]$	$[c_{gi}]$	$[c_{gf}]$
3	$[v_{fi}]$	$[v_{fg}]$		

The elements of each submatrix are technical input or output coefficients; they are defined concisely in the Mathematical Appendix, below.

While the input coefficients of ordinary goods can usually be derived from the observed flows, information on the magnitude of the structural coefficient describing the generation and elimination of pollutants has in most instances to be obtained directly from technological sources. Combined with appropriate figures of the outputs of all pollution-generating activities, these coefficients provide a basis for estimation of the pollution flows.

In many, not to say in most, instances pollution is being combated not through the operation of separate elimination processes, but rather through the use of less polluting alternative techniques for production of ordinary goods. To incorporate such additional information the structural matrix would have to describe the input structure of some industrial and possibly even of some final demand sectors in terms of several alternative columns of input and output coefficients. The corresponding flow tables would, and actually do already in many instances, show for some sectors two or more columns of input-output flows.

Without explaining in detail the mathematical formulation and solution of the system of input-output equations involved[1] it suffices here to say that on the basis of the information contained in an enlarged structural matrix of a given economy it would be possible to compute (and some such computations have already been made) the total factor inputs (measured in physical amounts or more or less

[1]See Mathematical Appendix; see also essay 6 in this volume; and Wassily Leontief and Daniel Ford, "Air Pollution and the Economic Structure: Empirical Results of Input-Output Computations," *Proceedings*, Fifth International Input-Output Conference (Amsterdam: North-Holland Publishing Co., 1972).

aggregated "value added" dollars) required directly and indirectly: (a) to deliver to final users one additional unit of any particular good while keeping the deliveries of all the other goods and the net outputs of all pollutants constant; (b) to reduce by one unit the *net* output of any particular pollutant while keeping constant the net outputs of all the other pollutants and final deliveries of all goods.

This means that factual information contained in an enlarged structural matrix of a particular economy would permit us to compute in a rough and ready fashion the opportunity costs of an additional unit of any good and of an eliminated unit of the "net output" of each pollutant. The basic matrix of structural coefficients that governs the physical flows presented on the enlarged input-output table determines also a corresponding set of price-cost relationships.

The elimination of pollutants originating in various sectors can be paid for either directly by the final users or by the producing sectors in which they are being generated. In the latter case the cost of doing so will obviously be included in the price of the finished product. I have explained elsewhere[2] how these institutionally determined parameters can be introduced in standard input-output formulation of balanced price-cost equations.

If the prices are expected to reflect the true opportunity costs of various goods (including the "products" of pollution-eliminating activities) to final users, they must cover the costs of eliminating all additional pollution generated in the process of their production. Otherwise in purchasing a useful good the consumer would receive, probably unwittingly, an additional delivery of undesirable pollutants. Hence, the system of prices to be used for purposes of welfare decisions should be computed on the assumption that each industry and each pollution-eliminating process bears the full cost of eliminating all pollutants generated by it. This of course does not imply that the actual institutional arrangement and consequently the actual pricing should necessarily be governed by the same principle, the more so that the distributional effect of such "pure" opportunity cost pricing might turn out to be undesirable.

Once the prices of all outputs (including those of all antipollution

[2]*Ibid.*

106

activities) have been determined, all entries in the expanded tables of interindustrial flows can be valued in dollars. Marginal totals can be entered not only at the end of each row but also at the bottom of each column. The outputs of all pollutants will be represented by negative dollar figures; the amounts of pollutants eliminated by positive dollar figures. In particular the net outputs of pollutants delivered to final users (2,4) will add up to a negative dollar figure. It can be interpreted as representing the upper limit of the amount that would have to be spent (but in fact was not spent) for this particular purpose if the final users decided to eliminate all pollution actually delivered to them.

Mathematical appendix

The numbering of goods, pollutants, and primary factors

$1, 2, \ldots, i, \ldots, j, \ldots, n$
$\quad n$ goods.
$n + 1, n + 2, \ldots, g, \ldots, k, \ldots, n + m$
$\quad m$ pollutants.
$n + m + 1, n + m + 2, \ldots, f, \ldots, n + m + h$
$\quad h$ primary factors.

Technical coefficients

a_{ij}—input of good i per unit of output of good j (produced by industry j).
a_{ig}—if > 0, input of good i per unit of eliminated pollutant g; if < 0, output of good i per unit of eliminated pollutant g.
a_{gi}—if > 0, output of pollutant g per unit of output of good i (produced by industry i); if < 0, input (productive use) of pollutant g per unit of output of good i (produced by industry i).
a_{gk}—output of pollutant g per unit of eliminated pollutant k.
c_{gi}—output of pollutant g generated in the final demand sector in the process of consuming one unit of good i.
c_{gf}—output of pollutant g generated in the final demand sector in the process of consuming one unit of the primary factor f.
v_{fi}—input of factor f per unit output of good i (produced by industry i).
v_{fg}—input of factor f per unit of eliminated pollutant g.
v_i—"value added" paid out by industry i per unit of its output.
v_g—"value added" paid out by the pollution-eliminating sector g per unit of pollution eliminated.

Vectors of technical coefficients

$[a_{ij}]$, $[a_{ig}]$, etc.

Variables

x_i—total output of good i by industry i.
x_g—total amount of pollutant g eliminated by pollutant-eliminating activity g.
x_f—total amount of factor f used in all sectors.
y_i—total amount of good i delivered to final demand.
y_g—*net* output of pollutant (delivered to final demand).
y_f—total amount of factor f delivered to final demand.
p_i—price of one unit of good produced by industry i.
p_g—price of eliminating one unit of pollution g by sector g.

Vectors of variables

$$
X_1 = \begin{bmatrix} x_1 \\ x_2 \\ \cdot \\ \cdot \\ \cdot \\ x_i \\ \cdot \\ \cdot \\ \cdot \\ x_j \\ \cdot \\ \cdot \\ \cdot \\ x_n \end{bmatrix}
\qquad
X_2 = \begin{bmatrix} x_{n+1} \\ x_{n+2} \\ \cdot \\ \cdot \\ \cdot \\ x_g \\ \cdot \\ \cdot \\ \cdot \\ x_k \\ x_{n+m} \end{bmatrix}
\qquad
X_3 = \begin{bmatrix} x_{n+m+1} \\ x_{n+m+2} \\ \cdot \\ \cdot \\ \cdot \\ x_f \\ \cdot \\ \cdot \\ \cdot \\ x_{n+m+h} \end{bmatrix}
$$

$$
Y_1 = \begin{bmatrix} y_1 \\ y_2 \\ \cdot \\ \cdot \\ \cdot \\ y_i \\ \cdot \\ \cdot \\ \cdot \\ y_j \\ \cdot \\ \cdot \\ \cdot \\ y_n \end{bmatrix}
\qquad
Y_2 = \begin{bmatrix} y_{n+1} \\ y_{n+2} \\ \cdot \\ \cdot \\ \cdot \\ y_g \\ \cdot \\ \cdot \\ \cdot \\ y_k \\ \cdot \\ \cdot \\ \cdot \\ y_{n+m} \end{bmatrix}
\qquad
Y_3 = \begin{bmatrix} y_{n+m+1} \\ y_{n+m+2} \\ \cdot \\ \cdot \\ \cdot \\ y_f \\ \cdot \\ \cdot \\ \cdot \\ y_{n+m+h} \end{bmatrix}
$$

$$V_1 = \begin{bmatrix} v_1 \\ v_2 \\ \cdot \\ \cdot \\ v_i \\ \cdot \\ \cdot \\ v_j \\ \cdot \\ \cdot \\ v_n \end{bmatrix} \quad V_2 = \begin{bmatrix} v_{n+1} \\ v_{n+2} \\ \cdot \\ \cdot \\ v_g \\ \cdot \\ \cdot \\ v_k \\ \cdot \\ \cdot \\ v_{n+m} \end{bmatrix} \quad P_1 = \begin{bmatrix} p_1 \\ p_2 \\ \cdot \\ \cdot \\ p_i \\ \cdot \\ \cdot \\ p_j \\ \cdot \\ \cdot \\ p_n \end{bmatrix} \quad P_2 = \begin{bmatrix} p_{n+1} \\ p_{n+2} \\ \cdot \\ \cdot \\ p_g \\ \cdot \\ \cdot \\ p_k \\ \cdot \\ \cdot \\ p_{n+m} \end{bmatrix}$$

Balance equations

Each of the following matrix equations describes the balance between the outputs and the inputs entered in one of the three row strips of the enlarged input-output table.

(1)
$$\begin{aligned}
\text{Goods} \quad & [I - a_{ij}] X_1 - [a_{ig}] X_2 = Y_2 \\
\text{Pollutants} \quad & -[a_{gi}] X_1 + [I - a_{gk}] X_2 = [c_{gi}] Y_1 - Y_2 + [c_{gf}] Y_3 \\
\text{Factors} \quad & -[v_{fi}] X_1 - [v_{fg}] X_2 + X_3 = Y_3
\end{aligned}$$

The general solution of that system for the unknown x's in terms of given y's is

(2)
$$\begin{bmatrix} X_1 \\ -- \\ X_2 \\ -- \\ X_3 \end{bmatrix} = \begin{bmatrix} [I - a_{ij}] & \vdots & -[a_{ig}] & \vdots & 0 \\ \cdots & \vdots & \cdots & \vdots & \cdots \\ -[a_{gi}] & \vdots & [I - a_{gk}] & \vdots & 0 \\ \cdots & \vdots & \cdots & \vdots & \cdots \\ -[v_{fi}] & \vdots & -[v_{fg}] & \vdots & [I] \end{bmatrix}^{-1} \begin{bmatrix} Y_1 \\ \cdots \\ [c_{gi}] Y_1 - Y_g + [c_{gf}] Y_3 \\ \cdots \\ Y_3 \end{bmatrix}$$

Separating the effects of the three kinds of outputs delivered to the final demand sector and expressing the relationship (2) in incremental terms:

(3)
$$\begin{bmatrix} \Delta X_1 \\ ---- \\ \Delta X_2 \\ --- \\ \Delta X_3 \end{bmatrix} = M \begin{bmatrix} \Delta Y_1 \\ ----- \\ [c_{gi}] \Delta Y_1 \\ ----- \\ 0 \end{bmatrix} + M \begin{bmatrix} 0 \\ ----- \\ -\Delta Y_2 \\ ----- \\ 0 \end{bmatrix} + M \begin{bmatrix} 0 \\ ----- \\ [c_{gf}] \Delta Y_3 \\ ----- \\ \Delta Y_3 \end{bmatrix}$$

The inverse of the enlarged structural matrix of the economy appearing on the right-hand side is the same that appears in (2) above.

The first and the third terms on the right-hand side describe the effect—on the output of goods (ΔX_1), the level of antipollution activities (ΔX_2), and total factor inputs

(ΔX_3)—of a given change in the final demand for goods (ΔY_1) and, respectively, final demand for primary factors (ΔY_2). These effects are computed on the assumption that the level of pollution-eliminating activities will be adjusted in such a way as to leave the net delivery of pollutants to final users unchanged (i.e., $\Delta Y_2 = 0$).

The second right-hand term shows what it would take—in total outputs of goods and total primary factor inputs—to *reduce* the delivery of (uneliminated) pollution to final users by the amount ΔY_2, while holding the deliveries of goods and factor services constant ($\Delta Y_1 = 0$, $\Delta Y_3 = 0$).

For purposes of price-cost computations, all primary factor flows entered along the second row-strip of the expanded input-output table can be valued in dollars and consolidated into a single row of "value added" figures. Accordingly the two coefficient matrices $-[v_{fi}]$ and $[v_{fg}]$ can be reduced to row vectors V_1 and V_2 of value-added coefficients.

If each industry and each antipollution activity were to pay—and include in the price of its product—the costs of eliminating all pollution directly generated by it,[3] the balance between revenues and outlays in all goods-producing and pollution-eliminating sectors could be described by the following matrix equations.

(4)
$$\begin{aligned} \text{Goods} \qquad & [I - a'_{ij}]P_1 - [a'_{gi}]P_2 = V_1 \\ \text{Pollutant elimination} \quad & [a'_{ig}]P_1 + [I - a'_{gk}]P_2 = V_2 \end{aligned}$$

The general solution of that system for unknown p's in terms of given v's is

(5)
$$\begin{bmatrix} P_1 \\ \hline P_2 \end{bmatrix} = \begin{bmatrix} [I - a'_{ij}] & -[a'_{gi}] \\ \hline -[a'_{ig}] & [I - a'_{gk}] \end{bmatrix}^{-1} \begin{bmatrix} V_1 \\ \hline V_2 \end{bmatrix}$$

[3]For price computations based on different assumptions see the article cited in notes 1 and 2.

VIII

An international comparison of factor costs and factor use

A REVIEW ARTICLE

For over 30 years—to be exact, since 1928—whenever a working economist was called on to describe in numbers or to interpret in analytical terms the relationship between the inputs of capital and labor and the final product of a plant, an industry, or a national economy as a whole, he was more likely than not to reach out for the Cobb-Douglas production function. Theorists questioned the arbitrariness of its form and statisticians the validity of procedures used in fitting it to given sets of data, but despite all criticism the familiar exponential equation was used over and over again, essentially, I think, because of its convenient simplicity. But now this remarkable career is apparently coming to an end. The old formula is being rapidly replaced by a new, improved recipe: the constant elasticity of substitution production function. In quantitative empirical analysis, the CES function can perform essentially the same role that the Cobb-Douglas function played up until now, but, owing to its less restrictive shape, it offers at the same time the indisputable advantage of greater flexibility.

In this monograph,[1] the new tool is used with considerable skill in a statistical inquiry designed to test—and, as it turns out, to disprove—one of the factual assumptions of the much-debated Hecksher-Ohlin interpretation of the classical theory of international

From *The American Economic Review*, Vol. 54, No. 4, June 1964.
[1]Bagicha Singh Minhas, *An International Comparison of Factor Costs and Factor Use*. Contributions to Economic Analysis, No. 31. Amsterdam: North-Holland Publishing Co., 1963.

trade. Mr. Minhas is one of the four joint authors—Professors Arrow, Chenery, and Solow are the others—of the article[2] published three years ago in which the CES function was not only described in some detail, but also, so far as I know, for the first time fitted to actual statistical data. Thus, it is not surprising to encounter in his book formulations and arguments already developed, or at least suggested, in that article.

The principal ideas are developed in four chapters which make up the first half of the book; the three remaining chapters are devoted to systematic statistical description and international comparison of the rates of return on capital in different industries. Presenting the results of what apparently first was conceived as a separate inquiry, the second half of the book bears only a loose, sketchily delineated relationship to the central line of argument developed in the first four chapters.

In a laudable endeavor to bring together theoretical and factual analysis, Minhas continuously shifts his argument from one to the other. For purposes of a critical review it seems to be more appropriate, after restating the substantive issue to which he addresses himself, to examine separately the new tool he chooses to use, the specific method of its application, and the interpretation of the results obtained.

The factual assumption of the modern theory of international trade that Minhas sets out to disprove is that a meaningful distinction can be made between capital- and labor-intensive industries, a distinction that incidentally plays a crucial role in analysis of economic development.

If the amounts of capital and of labor employed per unit of their respective outputs were technologically fixed, the ranking of different industries in accordance with the relative magnitude of the two input coefficients would certainly be valid. It still would be meaningful even if, in response to a given change in relative prices of the two factors, capital were substituted for labor or vice versa, provided the downward or the upward shifts of the capital-labor input ratios were so uniform as not to disturb to any significant extent the relative position of the individual industries on the capital-labor intensity scale. If, on the contrary, some industries responded to a given

[2]"Capital-Labor Substitution and Economic Efficiency," *Review of Economics and Statistics*, Aug. 1961, *43*, 225–50.

change in the relative price of the two factors by a much larger shift in their relative inputs than others, then their comparative position on the capital-labor intensity scale would often be reversed. The distinction between capital- and labor-intensive industries must lose in such a case much of its analytical usefulness. Neither in explanation of the pattern of international trade nor in the study of economic growth would it be permissible to utilize it as a technological datum. Minhas sets out to demonstrate empirically that this is actually the case, and he employs the constant elasticity of substitution production function to do so.

The constant elasticity of substitution—or as Minhas prefers to call it, the homohypallagic—production function can be written in the following form:

$$(1) \qquad V = (AK^{-\beta} + \alpha L^{-\beta})^{-1/\beta}$$

where V represents the output; K and L stand respectively for the inputs of capital and labor. Each one of the three quantities should be thought of as being measured in different physical units or, in the case of aggregative analysis, described by an appropriate index number. A, α, and β are constants which are supposed to reflect the technical characteristics of the particular production process. If K and L on the right-hand side of the formula are multiplied by an arbitrary positive constant, λ, the corresponding total output on the left-hand side will become $V\lambda$: this means that the production function described by equation (1) is homogeneous of the first degree; it obeys the law of constant returns to scale.

The partial derivatives of V in respect to L and K, i.e., the marginal productivities of labor and of capital, are:

$$(2a) \qquad \frac{\partial V}{\partial L} = \alpha \left(\frac{V}{L}\right)^{\beta+1} \qquad\qquad (2b) \qquad \frac{\partial V}{\partial K} = A \left(\frac{V}{K}\right)^{\beta+1}$$

and the marginal rate of substitution of capital for labor—let it be called x—is:

$$(3) \qquad x = \frac{\partial V}{\partial L} \bigg/ \frac{\partial V}{\partial K} = \frac{\alpha}{A} \left(\frac{K}{L}\right)^{\beta+1}$$

Translated into logarithmic terms, that equation describes a straight line:

$$(4) \qquad \log x = \log \frac{\alpha}{A} + (\beta + 1) \log \left(\frac{K}{L} \right).$$

Its constant slope $(\beta+1)$ is the reciprocal of the elasticity of substitution between capital and labor, σ:

$$(5) \qquad \sigma = d \log \left(\frac{K}{L} \right) \Big/ d \log x = \frac{1}{\beta+1}.$$

To demonstrate that the Cobb-Douglas production function represents a special case of the CES function in which $\sigma = 1$, i.e., $\beta = 0$, we can rewrite (3) interpreting its left-hand side as a derivative of K in respect to L along a constant output curve:

$$(6) \qquad \frac{dK}{dL} = -\frac{\alpha}{A} \frac{K}{L} \text{ or } -A \frac{dK}{K} = \alpha \frac{dL}{L}.$$

Integration of the two sides of the second expression gives:

$$(7) \qquad V = K^A L^\alpha$$

where the constant of integration, V, represents the output measured in appropriately defined units. After raising both sides of (1) to the power β, we can see that $A+\alpha=1$, if $\beta=0$, which is indeed the condition satisfied by the two exponents in the homogeneous Cobb-Douglas production function.

Perfect substitutability between capital and labor can also be interpreted as being a special case of the CES function (1): If $\sigma = \infty$ and consequently $\beta = -1$, it acquires the simple linear form,

$$(8) \qquad V = AK + \alpha L.$$

On a familiar two-dimensional graph the corresponding isoquants are represented by a set of negatively sloping parallel straight lines.

At the opposite extreme, when the elasticity of substitution tends toward 0 and β tends toward ∞, equation (1) degenerates into an input-output relationship characterized by constant capital and labor coefficients of production. However, for reasons that I will explain later, this rather special interpretation of a strictly complementary relation between capital and labor, though formally correct, is apt to be misleading when applied in statistical analysis of observed facts.

If a profit-maximizing industry considers the price of labor, w, and

114

the price of capital, r, as given, it will employ these two factors of production in such amounts as to equate the price ratio, $\dfrac{w}{r}$, to the marginal rate of substitution of capital for labor. According to (3) and (4), in the case of a CES function, the dependence of the factor input ratio, $\dfrac{K}{L}$, on the price ratio, $\dfrac{w}{r}$, is described by the simple log-linear relation,

$$(9) \qquad \log\left(\frac{w}{r}\right) = \log \frac{\alpha}{A} + (\beta + 1) \log \left(\frac{K}{L}\right).$$

Minhas illustrates his crucial argument concerning the possible effect of changing price ratios on the capital-labor input ratio in different industries by drawing the graph in Figure 1.

The two lines represent the relationship between the capital-labor ratio, $\dfrac{K}{L}$, and the relative price, $\dfrac{w}{r}$, in two different industries. The first industry will be more capital-intensive (and less labor-intensive) than

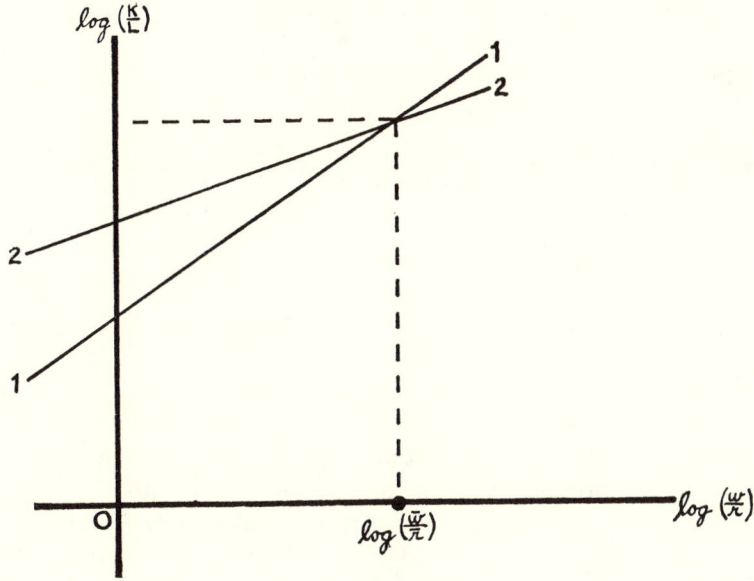

Figure 1

the second if the labor-capital price ratio happens to be higher than $\frac{\bar{w}}{\bar{r}}$, but the second will become more capital-intensive (and less labor-intensive) than the first if the labor-capital price ratio is lower than the critical level, $\frac{\bar{w}}{\bar{r}}$. The point A at which the two industries, while confronted with the same relative prices of capital and labor, would combine the two factors in exactly the same proportion is called by Minhas the crossover point. The position of the crossover depends on the slope $(\beta + 1)$ and the level $\left(\frac{\alpha}{A}\right)$ of each of the two curves. If the slopes of the two lines—that is, the elasticity of substitution between capital and labor in the two industries—happen to be exactly the same, the capital intensities of both industries will be identical throughout if the levels of both the lines happen to be also equal; otherwise, they will be parallel, which means that the capital-labor ratio in one of the two industries will be higher throughout than in the other. In case the elasticities are unequal, that is, the slopes of the two lines differ, they must necessarily intersect somewhere. The crossover points might, however, be located to the right or to the left of the usual or even possible range of observed capital-labor or price ratios. In this case, one industry can still be, for all practical purposes, unequivocally characterized as using more capital per unit of labor than the other.

Minhas sets out to demonstrate that, in fact, crossovers can be expected to occur within the practically relevant range so often as to vitiate the analytical usefulness of conventional distinctions between capital- and labor-intensive industries. I cannot agree with this and will now try to show that Minhas' own empirical evidence justifies the opposite conclusion.

To demonstrate the importance of the crossovers, Minhas, by a very ingenious procedure, fits CES production functions to 24 industries distributed over 19 different countries. The approach is cross-sectional; the primary data (presented in his Appendix I) consist of "value added produced per man year of labor input" and "annual wage rate payment per worker" compiled from official statistical publications for each industry in each country. Ingenuity is called for because no information on corresponding capital inputs or prices is used in the process. Values added, i.e., the gross revenues minus the costs of materials, are used throughout to represent the outputs, V. All wage rates and values added are converted to U.S. dollars in accordance with the fixed official or free market exchange rate.

On the assumption that the real wage rate paid equals the marginal productivity of labor, w can be substituted for $\dfrac{\partial V}{\partial L}$ on the left-hand side of (2a). The resulting equation can be written in the form of the following log-linear relationship:

$$(10) \qquad \log \left(\frac{V}{L}\right)_{ij} = \log a_i + b_i \log w_{ij}$$

where $\log a_i = -\log \alpha_i \dfrac{1}{\beta + 1}$ and $b_i = \dfrac{1}{\beta + 1} \equiv \sigma_i$.

Subscript i identifies the industry and subscript j the country. The constants, $\log a_i$ and b_i, carry only the industry but not the country subscript since the CES production function, the shape of which they are supposed to reflect, is assumed to be the same in all the countries.

The magnitude of parameters, $\log a_i$ and b_i, can thus be estimated by fitting a least-squares regression line through the scatter of $\log \left(\dfrac{V}{L}\right)_{ij}$ on $\log w_{ij}$, with a fixed i and varying j. The slope b_i of that regression line represents the elasticity of substitution between labor and capital in the ith industry. Among the 24 regression lines fitted by Minhas, the estimated magnitude of σ_i ranges from 0.7211 in Dairy Products to 1.0114 in Primary Nonferrous Metals; in 20 instances it exceeds 0.8, and in 8 of these it lies above 0.9.

To determine the location of potential "crossover" points marking the reversal in the relative capital-labor intensity of any two of the 24 industries, it is necessary to draw up for each one of them a log-linear relationship between $\dfrac{K}{L}$ and $\dfrac{w}{r}$ as described in equation (9) and shown in Figure 1. The elasticity of substitution between capital and labor determines, however, only the slope of the straight lines drawn on that graph. Their levels depend on the value of the two other constants, α_i and A_i, entering in the CES function of each industry, i. Equation (10) in addition to β_i (and, consequently, σ_{ij}) yields an estimate of α_i—the constant associated in the CES production function (1) with the labor input, L—but it is incapable of supplying also an estimate of A_i, which is the corresponding constant associated with the capital input, K.

To apply an analogous procedure in estimating the A's, it would be necessary only to replace the ratio $\dfrac{V}{L}$ on the left-hand side of (10) by the corresponding ratio $\dfrac{V}{K}$, and on its right-hand side replace the wage rate, w_{ij}, by r_{ij}, i.e., the rate of profit earned per unit of capital employed by industry i in country j.

Minhas presents the estimates of both the α's and the A's for only six of the many industries covered by his elasticity computations. The magnitudes of the α's and σ's entered in small Table IV correspond exactly to the least-squares estimates of these parameters—based on equation (10)—shown for all the 24 industries in his Tables I and II. No word is said, however, in explanation of the origin of the estimates of the six corresponding A's. This is the more surprising since the examination of the five "crossovers" between the capital-labor intensities of these particular six industries (shown on his Figures 5 and 6) constitutes the sole and only factual evidence that Minhas can cite in support of his sweeping and emphatic rejection of the conventional distinction between capital- and labor-intensive industries.

As I have said above, in Chapters 5 and 6, Minhas presents a rather detailed statistical analysis of the rates of return on capital invested in the same industries in different countries. Table XVII on page 92 summarizes the results of his inquiry; it covers 17 industries and five countries: United States, Canada, United Kingdom, Japan, and India. Most of the industries included in the larger set of data which Minhas actually uses to estimate two of the three parameters of the 24 CES production functions are represented directly or in slightly aggregated form also in Table XVII. The information contained in it can thus be used to estimate the missing third parameter for 17 of the 24 industries covered in his Table I. The two-step procedure I have used is described below.

Parameter A_i enters as denominator in the middle term of equation (9); for the purpose at hand it suffices to estimate for each industry the magnitude of that entire term, rather than of A_i alone. Equation (9) can be rewritten in the following form:

$$(9a) \qquad \log \left(\frac{\alpha_i}{A_i}\right) = \log \left(\frac{w_{ij}}{r_{ij}}\right) - (\beta_i + 1) \log \left(\frac{K_{ij}}{L_{ij}}\right).$$

In estimating the elasticities of substitution, Minhas has already obtained the magnitudes of the corresponding β_i's. He compiled and used in his computations the wage rates, w_{ij}; he also compiled—but apparently did not use for the same purpose—the r_{ij}'s for 17 industries in five countries.

The magnitude of the capital-labor ratio, $\left(\frac{K}{L}\right)_{ij}$, appearing in the second right-hand term of (9a), can be derived by combining the profit-rates data with information on wage rates and value added per worker, $\left(\frac{V}{L}\right)_{ij}$, which, as we have seen above, Minhas uses too. By his own assumption, the value added in any industry is exactly exhausted by payments to capital and labor employed by it: $V_{ij} = L_{ij} w_{ij} + K_{ij} r_{ij}$. Dividing both sides by $L_{ij} r_{ij}$ and rearranging the terms, we arrive at the following relationship:

$$(11) \qquad \left(\frac{K}{L}\right)_{ij} = \left(\frac{V}{L}\right)_{ij} \frac{1}{r_{ij}} - \frac{w_{ij}}{r_{ij}}.$$

With all the magnitudes appearing to the right of the equation sign given, we can compute $\left(\frac{K}{L}\right)_{ij}$. Inserted on the right-hand side of (9a), this completes the information required to determine the magnitude of the constant, $\log \left(\frac{\alpha}{A}\right)_i$.

I have performed these additional computations for 21 of the 24 industries covered in Minhas' study, all those industries for which his Table XVII supplies an estimate of the rate of return on capital, r_{ij}. The results are shown in Figure 2. The factor price ratios, $\frac{w_{ij}}{r_{ij}}$, inserted in the course of these computations in equation (11) are those recorded for the industry in question in the United States. This means that the magnitude of the constant term, $\log \left(\frac{\alpha}{A}\right)_i$, was determined so as to make each one of the straight lines shown on Figure 2 pass

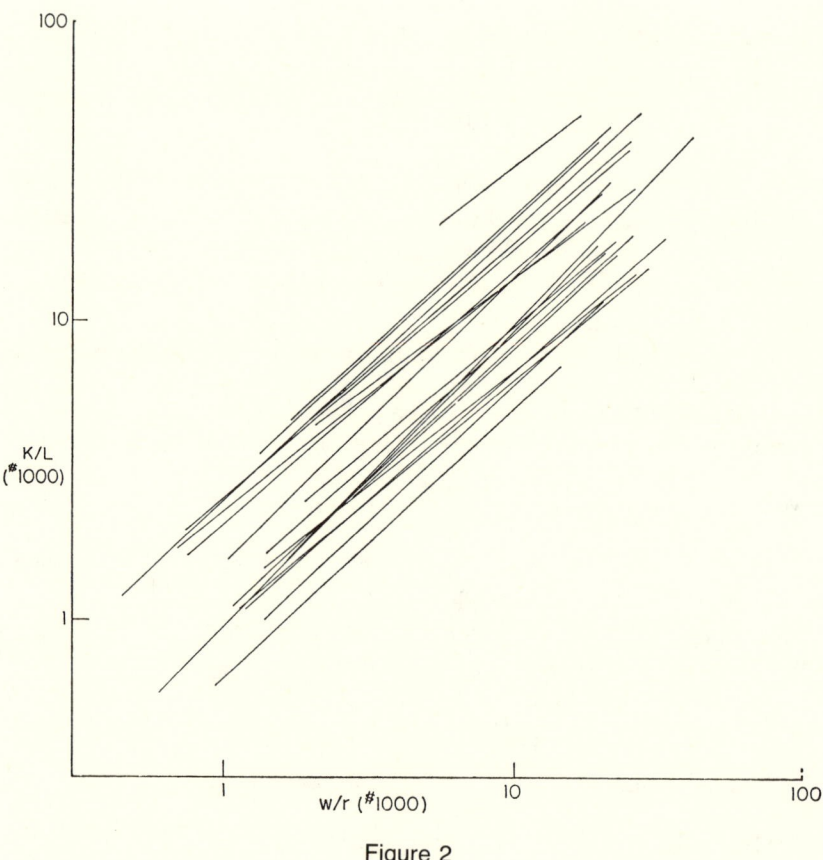

Figure 2

exactly through the point describing the combination of factor prices and factor inputs actually recorded for that particular industry in the United States. As should have been expected, all these points are located at the upper right-hand ends of all the 21 corresponding lines. The lowest of the $\left(\dfrac{K}{L}\right)_{ij}$ ratios observed in any industry i—typically observed in India—determine the cutoff at the lower left-hand end of each line. The corresponding lowest factor price ratios, $\left(\dfrac{w}{r}\right)_i$, would have been equal to the wage-profit ratio actually observed in India if the theoretical assumption on which these computations are based were faultless and the empirical information error-free. In fact, the

120

actual ratios deviate, of course, from those predicted on the assumption that the U.S. price and input ratios lie exactly on the curve.

The picture emerging from supplemental computations as shown in Figure 2 does not confirm Minhas' emphatically stated conclusion that "the strong factor intensity assumption, the conventional distinction between capital and labor intensive industries is of limited practical validity." On the contrary, it seems to confirm the conventional view. Of the theoretically possible 210 crossover points between the 21 lines entered on the graph, only 17 are found to be located within the wide range of factor price ratios, spanned on the one end by those observed in the United States and on the other by those reported from India. Moreover, most of these crossovers occur between industries whose curves run so close together throughout the entire range that for all practical purposes their capital-labor intensities would be considered identical. With two or three exceptions, each one of the 21 industries represented can be characterized as capital-intensive, labor-intensive, or as belonging to an intermediate group. In the light of this evidence the modern theory of international trade stands vindicated.

To avoid undesirable confusion of related but separable issues, up to this point I have presented Minhas' arguments and examined his conclusions without questioning the general theoretical framework within which they have been set. Interested in demonstrating the practical importance of crossovers, he naturally rejected the Cobb-Douglas function—which excludes crossovers by definition—and reached out for a formula capable of showing their existence. But if this were the principal reason for acquiring one more degree of freedom, the result of my extended computations shown in Figure 2 could easily justify a return to the simpler Cobb-Douglas formula. This suggestion would appear to be even more plausible if in applying the least-squares method to estimate the slopes, b_i, in the log-linear equations (10), Minhas had not proceeded on the assumption that only the variable $\left(\dfrac{V}{L}\right)_i$ is subject to random errors, while the variable w_i is not. Had he instead, in fitting the slopes of these regression lines, allowed also for errors affecting the observed magnitudes of w_i, all estimated elasticities would necessarily turn out to be larger, since in 23 out of the 24 industries examined by him, the magnitudes of the b_i's, i.e., the elasticities of substitution, turn out to be less—although in most instances only slightly less—than 1. This means that their values would be still closer to 1—the constant elasticity of the Cobb-Douglas function.

The inverse proportionality (implied by $b_i = 1$) between the number of workers employed per unit of output of a particular industry and the wage rate paid to them by that industry in different countries can be explained in entirely different terms. The assumption that a man-year of labor in one part of the world is equivalent to a man-year of labor in any other part, i.e., that the typical worker employed, say, in India is equal in productive efficiency to his similarly employed counterpart in the United States, can be questioned. If such equivalence were the rule rather than an exception, why should economists studying problems of economic development be so much concerned with investment—or rather the lack of it—in "human capital"?

Let it be assumed, for argument's sake, that an average man-year of labor employed by a given industry in one country is twice as efficient as a man-year employed by the same industry in another country. The production function in both instances can still appear to be, and actually will be, essentially the same, provided that, in measuring labor inputs for purposes of comparison, we multiply the figure describing the amount of labor absorbed by that industry in the first country by 2. At the same time, for comparison of the real unit costs of labor to that industry, the actual annual wage rate paid by it in the first country would have to be divided by 2. Such a procedure would be analogous to that used by Ricardo in his theory of rent. He visualized an agricultural production function allowing for several different grades of land and explained the higher price paid for an acre of better land by its proportionally greater efficiency. A similar argument was used recently by Houthakker when he interpreted the difference in the unit price paid by consumers for grades of nominally the same article as a measure of intrinsic qualitative difference.

The elasticity which Minhas estimates by fitting equation (10) to cross-section data measures—if it is interpreted in this sense—not substitution between capital and labor but rather substitution between different grades of labor, or possibly some combination of both. In the first case, the magnitude of the elasticity constant, b_i, in equation (10), as estimated by him, would necessarily be close to 1.

To determine which interpretation of Minhas' findings is correct, it is necessary to bring information on capital inputs explicitly into the picture. An elaborate comparison of rates of return on capital in different industries and countries can be found in the last two chapters. As I said above, the author nevertheless relies exclusively on the elegant but, even for his own purposes, not sufficiently powerful procedure in the course of which the elasticity of substitution between capital and labor is derived on the basis of information pertaining to labor only.

I have performed the simple numerical manipulations (similar to those described above in connection with the construction of my Figure 2) required to determine the capital-output ratios, $\left(\dfrac{K}{V}\right)_{ij}$, that would match the labor-output ratios, $\left(\dfrac{L}{V}\right)_{ij}$, used in Minhas' own computations. An examination of the resulting scatters shows that, as compared to the corresponding labor intensity, the capital intensity of any given industry varies little from country to country, and only in a few instances could one discern a visible negative relationship between the two. The overall picture is thus quite different from that which emerges from what Minhas calls the straightforward, but which in fact is a rather one-sided, method of estimating the elasticity of substitution between capital and labor.

In the light of closer examination of empirical evidence, fixed capital and labor coefficients (the latter measured in comparable efficiency units) might after all prove to be more appropriate for description of the specific productive relationships than the CES function in its general, or its particular Cobb-Douglas, form.

Judging by the practical implication that Minhas draws from it, the formally correct interpretations of fixed capital and labor coefficients as a special case of the CES function tend to be misleading. Fixed coefficients of production can be interpreted more meaningfully as representing a special case of technological conditions under which the two factors can be substituted for each other, but only within relatively narrow limits: the rate of substitution of capital for labor decreasing sharply and approaching zero whenever the capital-labor input ratio approaches a finite upper limit, but falling and becoming infinitely large when that ratio approaches the—also finite—lower limit. The elasticity-of-substitution concept proves to be a very awkward tool for analyzing this type of situation, and the assumption of constant elasticity of substitution simply breaks down in such a case. If the upper and lower limits of the admissible capital-labor input ratios lie comparatively close together, the average fixed coefficients will give an adequate description of such a technology. A combination of two or more alternative sets of such coefficients would of course do still better.

Except in its degenerate form when $\sigma = 0$, the CES function itself represents, as a matter of fact, a special case of homogeneous production characterized by literally unlimited substitution possibilities between factors, thus implying—when these factors are capital and labor—that any amount of a finished product can be obtained with a practically negligible amount of either capital or labor provided the supply of the other factors is large enough. This might be a good enough assumption in aggregative analysis where all possible products and processes of production are subsumed under a single loosely defined production function describing not so much a substitution of one method of production for another as a changing product mix. It is, however, hardly adequate for description of alternative input structures of sharply defined individual industries.

The length of this review testifies to the amount of stimulation an interested reader can find in this slim volume. The questions which the author asks are so well put that they will advance the understanding of factor use by the various branches of production in an international setting even if some of the answers which he gives cannot be accepted.

IX

Explanatory power of the comparative cost theory of international trade and its limits

Old well-established truths need to be from time to time reexamined. On a second or a third inspection some of their implications might turn out different from what one remembers them to be.

The theory of comparative costs[1] is often assumed to be capable—in principle at least and with proper empirical implementation—of explaining the network of interregional trade flows. The magnitude and the direction of these flows is supposed to depend on the specific combinations of capital, labor, and other primary resources possessed by each one of the trading countries, the shapes of the production and consumption functions, i.e., the alternative input-output combinations that can actually be used in each country to transform primary resources and intermediate products (some of which will also be imported or exported) into final goods, and the valuation of alternative combinations of these goods by different groups of potential consumers.

Perusal of empirical studies concerned with the explanation of bilateral trade flow between two or several countries or groups of countries leaves no doubt that behind such specific quantitative explanations lies very often the belief that all such analysis can indeed be firmly rooted in the formal framework of the comparative cost theory referred to above.

From *Economic Structure and Development* (Amsterdam: North-Holland Publishing Co.; and New York: American Elsevier Publishing Co., 1973), pp. 153–60.

[1]An excellent exposition and discussion of several of its most recent versions can be found in Paul Samuelson [1].

Actually this is not so, except in very special instances. Only to the extent to which transportation costs, customs tariffs, or any other differential transfer costs between the individual trading countries can actually be taken into account and happen to be of decisive importance, will the comparative cost theory be capable of explaining the magnitude and the composition of all the observed export-import flows. In case such differential transfer costs do not exist or if they do exist but cannot be accounted for, the magnitude and composition of the flow of goods or services from any one to any other country remain within the framework of such theory entirely indeterminate.

To demonstrate that this is actually so let us visualize the trading countries being represented by players sitting around a table and the goods that they are trading by chips of as many different colors as there are different kinds of such goods.

Given the quantities of primary resources possessed by each country, the set of production technologies among which it actually can choose, as well as conditions determining the structure of each country's final demand for various goods, the comparative cost theory provides a systematic means of determining, i.e., of explaining how many chips of different colors each individual player will be prepared to give away to all the other players in exchange for specified amounts of chips of other colors received from them. How the theory determines these amounts is strictly speaking irrelevant to the present argument; it suffices to know that the answer it provides will satisfy the condition that the aggregate number of chips of a particular color "supplied" by all the players giving them away will be exactly equal to the total number of chips of that particular color "demanded" by those who would want to receive them.

The actual transaction can be visualized as being accomplished in two steps supervised by a croupier. First he collects the chips given away by all the players and sorts them out in piles of different colors. Next he deals from each pile the number of chips of that color which according to the comparative cost solution various players are entitled to receive. At the end of that second round the piles in the middle of the table will be gone and each player will have given away and received as many chips of each color as he wanted to.

Now let us introduce into this procedure an additional step: before handing over to the croupier the chips which he decided to give away each player will write his name on the back of them. In receiving, piling up, and dealing out the chips to the individual players the croupier will handle them so as to keep the reverse sides down. Only after the entire transaction has been completed will each player be asked to turn the chips received by him reverse-side up. On the basis of the additional information thus revealed the croupier will then construct a transaction table showing how many chips of a particular color have been "traded" by any one player to any other player.

Now let us ask whether, if this game were repeated many times without any change in any of the basic factors determining the "comparative costs" position of all the players, the figures entered on the transaction table constructed at the end of each round would remain the same? Certainly they would not. The *total* number of chips of one particular color "exported" and "imported" by each country would of course remain the same, but their *distribution* by countries of destination, or respectively of origin, would change from one round of the game to the next in a random fashion. Translated back into economics' language this means that so long as transportation and other transfer costs are not taken into account, the comparative cost theory cannot explain why a particular amount of this or that good is exported to or imported from this or that particular country. Within the limits set by given aggregate amounts of each type of good exported or imported, as the case may be, by each of the trading countries, the country-to-country flows remain completely indetermined.

If all transfer costs were zero, a great many—strictly speaking infinitely many—different interregional trade patterns could satisfy all the minimization and maximization criteria inherent in the application of the comparative cost principle equally well. Any attempt to explain why West Germany is for example exporting more chinaware to Italy than to France or why the United States buys more oil from Venezuela than from Iran would be futile.

In fact the transfer costs of course hardly ever equal zero and the optimal trading pattern can in principle at least be uniquely determined by minimizing their sum total. However, if such costs represent a relatively small fraction of the total costs of the internationally traded goods the formally unique optimal trading pattern would be as sensitive to small random shock as the position of a billiard ball placed on a flat marble table.

While speaking of transfer costs, I really have in mind *differential* transfer costs since only the differences between the costs of, for example, moving coal, say, from the United States to France, to Japan, to Italy, or to any of the other coal importing countries can affect the regional distribution of the U.S. coal exports. In the game described above, if a special but equal charge were to be paid by the American player for each coal-black chip laid down by him on or scooped up by him from the table the entire comparative cost solution would of course be affected, but the country-to-country flows of the black as well as of all the other chips would remain as indetermined as they were before.

This means that the so-called terminal costs have to be omitted from any comparison of differential transfer costs. Loading costs can for example not affect the differences between shipping a particular good from any given port to one or to another port, neither can the unloading charges affect differences between the cost of importing goods from one or from another country. The same is true of course of import duties subject to the "most favored nations" clause that bars an importing country from varying the height of a levy imposed on a given type of good according to the country of its origin.

Turning from theory to observed facts we find that information contained in the U.S. input-output table for 1963 shows that in that year the combined transportation and insurance margins constituted 7.5 percent and custom duties 7.2 percent of the aggregate value of imports (at domestic ports).

Since the great bulk of trade was covered by the most favored nations clause, the duties however did not constitute part of differential transfer costs. A very large proportion of internationally traded goods is moved over the water. Closer examination of the transportation margins shows (see the appendix) that terminal charges, which affect all incoming cargoes irrespective of their origin and outgoing cargoes irrespective of their destination, constitute as much as 85 percent (for conventional ships) and not less that 50 percent (for container ships) of the total transportation costs in trans-Atlantic and in trans-Pacific trade of the United States; insurance costs also depend to a large extent on conditions prevailing at points of origin and destination points rather than time or distance that separates them from each other.

All in all differential transfer costs constitute but a small fraction of the total value of most internationally traded goods. Hence while the assumption of zero differential transfer cost is strictly speaking invalid, so far as the applicability or rather the nonapplicability of the comparative cost theory in explanation of the actually observed international trade pattern is concerned the theoretical implications of this assumption can be expected to be practically true. Such an explanation has to be consequently sought in quotas, discriminatory duties, and other preferential arrangements of a formal or informal kind.

In a special case in which either the total international supply of or the entire demand for a particular good is concentrated in a single country the origin as well as the destination of all its shipments will obviously be uniquely determined. The question does not even arise in the simple textbook example (usually illustrated by a graph) in which the world is assumed to consist of only two countries.

In connection with what has been said above, it might be worthwhile to remember that the explanatory power of comparative cost theory turns out to be even more restricted in the actually hardly ever existing, but theoretically much discussed, case of international factor price equalization. The well-known Samuelson-Stolper theorem states that under certain conditions the free, unimpeded international exchange would equalize not only the price of goods and services actually sold and purchased across national borders, but also of the so-called primary factors of production such as labor, capital, and natural resources.

Without entering into the detail of the theoretical argument it suffices to observe that such international factor price equalization could occur if the total number of goods were larger than the number of primary factors and if all countries had free access to the same production techniques. Under such conditions one can visualize a state in which each good is being produced throughout the entire world with the same input combination of primary factors (per unit of output) and at the same time different industries are distributed between the different countries in such a way as to make full use of the particular combinations of primary resources available in each one of them. The national surpluses and deficits of goods would be of course balanced out—as in the game described above—through trade. No reason would exist in such a state for pricing any factor in one country higher or lower than in any other country.

In the discussion of the factor price equalization theorem however it is not often enough emphasized that under the (obviously quite unrealistic) set of conditions described above, not only one, but many alternative distributions of industrial activities between different countries could yield the same combination of aggregate world outputs of all goods while satisfying at the same time the requirement of full utilization of all primary resources that happen to be available in each country. This means that under such conditions and in the absence of international transfer costs not only the network of country-to-country commodity flow, but even the level and the composition of each country's total exports and imports (in our example—the total number of chips of different colors offered and received by each player) could not be uniquely determined.

In case the interregional transfer costs are known, their minimization, combined with the comparative costs conditions mentioned above, can lead to determination of a unique optimal output pattern for each country as well as of its total export or total import of each type of goods. In case transfer costs consisted only of terminal charges and thus had not depended on the length and direction of various transportation routes, the bilateral intercountry trading pattern would still of course be indetermined.

The theorists who formulate and reformulate the theory of comparative costs are certainly aware of what it can and what it cannot be expected to explain; they often fail however to emphasize its limitations to those who might want to use it in empirical research or in defense of particular specific policy decisions.

Appendix

1. The breakdown of international transfer costs of goods imported by the United States in the year 1963 as derived from the official U.S. input-output data for that year is presented in Table 1.

Those figures cover some 90 percent of total U.S. merchandise imports. The remaining 10 percent consist of so-called noncompetitive imports such as coffee, tin, and other agricultural and mineral products not produced in the United States. The margins on these products are about the same as those on imports included in the table.

2. Available shipping data strongly support the contention that international freight costs are largely invariate with route length. Estimates in Table 2 attribute

Table 1—1963 United States merchandise imports by industrial sector:
domestic port values and tariff, freight and insurance margins
(percentage of domestic port value)

SECTOR	DOMESTIC PORT VALUE ($1,000)	TARIFF MARGIN (%)	FREIGHT MARGIN (%)	INSURANCE MARGIN (%)
Agriculture	1224.3	7.0	9.9	0.5
Iron ore	533.2	1.6	19.0	0.1
Nonferrous ores	425.5	1.6	3.0	0.2
Coal	2.2	0.0	0.0	0.0
Oil	1340.3	3.2	18.2	0.6
Mining	233.3	2.0	13.8	0.3
Food	2569.7	7.7	5.0	0.3
Tobacco	4.5	16.3	3.7	0.3
Textiles	970.5	13.5	4.5	0.7
Apparel	507.9	20.6	4.5	0.5
Wood	502.9	1.5	9.6	0.8
Lumber	307.2	11.6	10.4	0.9
Furniture	40.3	11.3	8.0	0.3
Paper	1168.9	1.2	3.3	1.0
Printing	71.4	4.1	6.5	0.3
Chemical products	401.5	8.2	5.9	0.6
Plastics	71.3	13.5	3.8	0.3
Heavy chemicals	78.8	12.0	2.5	0.5
Paint	0.7	0.0	14.3	0.0
Petroleum products	935.2	2.3	9.7	0.7
Rubber	182.3	11.3	4.2	0.7
Leather	225.2	12.4	4.9	0.4
Glass	202.0	20.5	6.4	0.4
Stone products	130.0	8.3	8.0	0.9
Steel	825.2	5.8	6.9	0.7
Nonferrous metals	1168.8	3.2	1.8	0.4
Structural metals	5.5	14.5	5.5	3.6
Metal products	276.3	10.4	3.7	0.6
Engines	29.2	7.9	1.9	0.7
Machines, specialized	357.2	4.8	3.1	0.7
Metalworking machines	72.7	13.1	1.8	0.3
Machines, general purpose	62.5	11.4	2.5	0.7
Machines, office	115.7	6.9	2.6	0.6
Heavy electric machines	48.5	9.7	5.0	0.4
Heavy appliances	214.2	9.7	3.8	0.9
Electronics	350.8	9.4	4.2	0.9
Motor vehicles	645.3	6.6	5.3	0.4
Aircraft	101.1	2.1	2.1	1.0
Transport equipment	111.9	10.4	5.0	0.6
Precision instruments	142.7	25.0	2.4	0.5
Photo optical	149.1	13.3	3.3	0.6
Miscellaneous manufactures	934.0	16.8	4.4	0.6
Total	17319.5	7.2	6.9	0.6

Source: The table was compiled by Peter Petri from information supplied by the Office of Business Economics, U.S. Department of Commerce.

Table 2—Terminal charges as a percentage of total U.S. freight revenue, by carrier type, 1964 and 1965

CARRIER TYPE	1964	1965
Tramp service	88	72
Liner service	74	70
Tanker service	56	60
Total	74	69

Source: James R. Barker and Robert Brandwein [2].

Table 3—Itemized freight cost breakdown for typical conventional and container ships, in percent

COST ITEM	CONVENTIONAL SHIP	CONTAINER SHIP
Costs variable with route length		
Crew	6.3	3.8
Fuel	2.2	5.5
Costs not variable with route length		
Capital costs	8.5	22.8
Maintenance	1.5	4.2
Port charges	2.0	1.5
Administrative	2.1	7.5
Cargo-handling	77.3	54.7
Total	100.0	100.0

Source: United Nations [3].

nearly three-fourths of U.S. freight revenues to terminal charges—mainly port dues and stevedore services.

An itemized freight cost breakdown for conventional and container ships appears in Table 3. These estimates are based upon typical values of vessel capacity, performance, and construction cost.

References

1. P. Samuelson, "Ohlin Was Right," *Swedish Journal of Economics* 73, No. 4 (Dec. 1971) pp. 365–384.
2. J. R. Barker and R. Brandwein, *The United States Merchant Marine in National Perspective* (D.C. Heath and Co., Lexington, Mass., 1970) p. 226.
3. Unitization of cargo, United Nations Conference on Trade and Development (U.N., New York, 1970).

X

Structure of the world economy

OUTLINE OF A SIMPLE INPUT-OUTPUT FORMULATION

I

The world economy, like the economy of a single country, can be visualized as a system of interdependent processes. Each process, be it the manufacture of steel, the education of youth, or the running of a family household, generates certain outputs and absorbs a specific combination of inputs. Direct interdependence between two processes arises whenever the output of one becomes an input of the other: coal, the output of the coal mining industry, is an input of the electric power generating sector. The chemical industry uses coal not only directly as a raw material but also indirectly in the form of electrical power. A network of such links constitutes a system of elements which depend upon each other directly, indirectly, or both.

The state of a particular economic system can be conveniently described in the form of a two-way input-output table showing the flows of goods and services among its different sectors, and to and from processes or entities ("value added" and "final demand") viewed as falling outside the conventional borders of an input-output system. As the scope of the inquiry expands, new rows and columns are added to the table and some of the external inflows and outflows become internalized. Increasing the number of rows and columns that de-

Nobel Memorial Lecture. © The Nobel Foundation, 1974; published in *The Swedish Journal of Economics*, Vol. 76, 1974.

The author is indebted to Peter Petri for setting up and performing all the computations, the results of which are presented in this lecture, and to D. Terry Jenkins for preparing the graphs and editorial assistance.

scribe an economic system also permits a more detailed description of economic activities commonly described in highly aggregative terms.

Major efforts are presently underway to construct a data base for a systematic input-output study not of a single national economy but of the world economy viewed as a system composed of many interrelated parts. This global study, as described in the official document, is aimed at

> helping Member States of the United Nations make their 1975 review of world progress in accelerating development and attacking mass poverty and unemployment. First, by studying the results that prospective environmental issues and policies would probably have for world development in the absence of changes in national and international development policies, and secondly, by studying the effects of possible alternative policies to promote development while at the same time preserving and improving the environment. By thus indicating alternative future paths which the world economy might follow, the study would help the world community to make decisions regarding future development and environmental policies in as rational a manner as possible.[1]

Preliminary plans provide for a description of the world economy in terms of 28 groups of countries, with about 45 productive sectors for each group. Environmental conditions will be described in terms of 30 principal pollutants; the use of nonagricultural natural resources in terms of some 40 different minerals and fuels.

II

The subject of this lecture is the elucidation of a particular input-output view of the world economy. This formulation should provide a framework for assembling and organizing the mass of factual data needed to describe the world economy. Such a system is essential for a concrete understanding of the structure of the world economy as well as for a systematic mapping of the alternative paths along which it could move in the future.

Let us consider a world economy consisting of (1) a Developed and

[1] Quoted from: "Brief Outline of the United Nations Study on the Impact of Prospective Environmental Issues and Policies on the International Development Strategy," April 1973.

Table 1—World economy in 1970 (billions of 1970 dollars)

Developed Countries

	Extraction Industry	Other Production	Abatement Industry	Final Demand		Total Output
				Domestic	Trade	
Extraction Industry	0	76	0	2	−15	63
Other Production	21	1809	21	2414	19	4284
Pollution	5	62	−63	60	0	64
Employ-ment	18	1372	20	287	0	
Other Value Added	21	996	22	0	0	

Less Developed Countries

	Extraction Industry	Other Production	Abatement Industry	Final Demand		Total Output
				Domestic	Trade	
Extraction Industry	0	8	0	2	15	25
Other Production	7	197	0	388	−19	573
Pollution	2	8	0	11	0	21
Employ-ment	9	149	0	99	0	
Other Value Added	8	220	0	0	0	

(2) a Less Developed region. Let us further divide the economy of each region into three productive sectors: an Extraction Industry producing raw materials; All Other Production, supplying conventional goods and services; and a Pollution Abatement Industry. In addition to these three sectors, there is also a consumption sector specified for each region. The function of the Abatement Industry is to eliminate pollutants generated by the productive sectors, consumers, and the Abatement Industry itself.

The two input-output tables displayed as Table 1 describe the intersectoral flows of goods and services within the Developed and the Less Developed economies. The flow of natural resources from the Less Developed to the Developed Countries, as well as the opposite flow of Other Goods from the Developed to the Less Developed Countries are entered in both tables: positively for the exporting region, and negatively for the importing region.

In each of the two tables the right-most entries in the first and second row represent the total domestic outputs of the Extraction Industry and of Other Production, respectively.

Each positive number along the third (pollution) row shows the physical amount of pollutant generated by the activity named at the head of the column in which that number appears. The negative quantity shown at the intersection of the third column and the third row represents the amount of pollutant eliminated by Abatement activities. Inputs such as power, chemicals, etc., purchased by the Abatement Industry from other sectors, and value added paid out by that industry are entered as positive amounts in the same third column. The difference between the total amount of pollution generated in all sectors and the amount eliminated by the Abatement sector is represented by the *net* emission figure, the right-most entry in the third row. Finally, labor inputs used in each sector and payments made to other income-receiving agents are shown in the bottom two rows.

The numbers in these two tables are, strictly speaking, fictitious. But their general order of magnitude reflects crude, preliminary estimates of intersectoral flows within and between the Developed and Less Developed regions during the past decade.[2]

For analytical purposes, the outputs and inputs of the Extraction Industry and Other Production, as well as the amounts of pollutants generated and abated, can be interpreted as quantities measured in the appropriate physical units (pounds, yards, kilowatts, etc.). The same is true of the services of some of the so-called primary factors: labor inputs, for example, are entered in the second to last row of each table. A similar physical measurement of the other components of value added, even if it were possible in principle, is impossible given the present state of knowledge. In pure or, should I say, speculative economic theory, we can overcome this kind of difficulty by introducing some convenient albeit unrealistic assumptions. But a theoretical formulation designed to permit empirical analysis has to account for the fact that at least some components of value added cannot be interpreted as payments for measurable physical inputs, but must be treated as purely monetary magnitudes.

[2] All quantities are measured in billions of dollars "in current prices"; pollutants are "priced" in terms of average "per unit" abatement costs.

The flows described in the two input-output tables are interdependent. They have to satisfy three distinct sets of constraints. First, within each production or consumption process there exists a technological relationship between the level of output and the required quantities of various inputs. For example, if we divide each figure in the first column of the first section of Table 1 (the inputs of the Extraction Industry) by the total output of that sector (the last figure in the first row), we find that to produce one unit of its output this sector absorbed 0.3372 units of the output of Other Production, used 0.2867 units of Labor Services and spent 0.3332 dollars for other value added. Moreover, for each unit of useful output the Extraction Industries generated 0.0859 units of pollution. Other sets of input-output coefficients describe the technical structure of every sector of production and consumption in both groups of countries.

While statistical input-output tables continue to serve as the principal source of information on the input requirements or "cooking recipes" of various industries, increasingly we find economists using engineering data as a supplemental source. Complete structural matrices of the two groups of countries used in our example are shown in Table 2.

Table 2—Technical and consumption coefficients[a]

Developed countries

$$A_1 = \begin{bmatrix} .0 & .0178 & .0 \\ .3372 & .4223 & .3298 \\ .0859 & .0144 & .0118 \end{bmatrix} \qquad C_1 = \begin{bmatrix} .0007 \\ .8834 \\ .0218 \end{bmatrix}$$

$$l_1 = [.2867 \quad .3203 \quad .3161] \qquad l_1^c = [.1050]$$

$$r_1 = [.3332 \quad .2324 \quad .3482] \qquad r_1 = [.0 \quad]$$

Less developed countries

$$A_2 = \begin{bmatrix} .0 & .0141 & .0 \\ .2934 & .3437 & .3298 \\ .0859 & .0144 & .0118 \end{bmatrix} \qquad C_2 = \begin{bmatrix} .0037 \\ .7943 \\ .0218 \end{bmatrix}$$

$$l_2 = [.3729 \quad .2597 \quad .3161] \qquad l_2^c = [.2020]$$

$$r_2 = [.3337 \quad .3825 \quad .3541] \qquad r_2' = [.0 \quad]$$

[a]The coefficients in these tables do not sum to unity because the pollution generated by industry and by final demand is only partially abated in the developed countries and not abated at all in the less developed countries.

The second set of constraints that has to be satisfied by every viable system requires that the total (physical) amounts of outputs and inputs of each type of good must be in balance, i.e., total supply must equal total demand. In the case of a pollutant, *net* emission must equal the total amount generated by all sectors less the amount eliminated by the abatement process.

For example, the balance between the total output and the combined inputs of extracted raw materials can be described by the following equation:

(1)

$$\underbrace{(1-a_{11})x_1}_{\substack{\text{net output}\\\text{of Extrac-}\\\text{tion In-}\\\text{dustry}}} - \underbrace{a_{12}x_2}_{\substack{\text{amount}\\\text{delivered}\\\text{to Other}\\\text{Production}}} - \underbrace{a_{13}x_3}_{\substack{\text{amount}\\\text{delivered}\\\text{to the}\\\text{Abatement}\\\text{Industry}}} - \underbrace{c_1y}_{\substack{\text{amount}\\\text{delivered}\\\text{to Final}\\\text{Users}}} - \underbrace{T_1}_{\substack{\text{amount}\\\text{exported}}} = 0$$

The equation describing the balance between generation, abatement and net emission of pollution reads as follows:

(2)

$$\underbrace{-a_{31}x_1 - a_{32}x_2}_{\substack{\text{gross amount}\\\text{of pollution}\\\text{generated by}\\\text{sectors 1 and 2}}} + \underbrace{(1-a_{33})x_3}_{\substack{\text{amount}\\\text{abated by}\\\text{abatement}\\\text{activities}}} - \underbrace{c_3y}_{\substack{\text{gross amount}\\\text{generated by}\\\text{consumers}\\\text{and govern-}\\\text{ment}}} + \underbrace{E}_{\substack{\text{net amount}\\\text{emitted into}\\\text{the environ-}\\\text{ment}}} = 0$$

x_1 and x_2 represent the total outputs of the Extraction Industry and of Other Production respectively; x_3, the level of activity of the Abatement sector; y, the sum total of values added, i.e., gross national income. The "technical coefficient" a_{ij} represents the number of units of the product of sector i absorbed (or generated in the case of pollution) by sector j in producing one unit of its output; c_j is a "consumption coefficient" describing the number of units of the output of sector j consumed (or generated in the case of pollution) per unit of total value added, i.e., per unit of gross national income.

Table 3

Physical subsystem

Equation number	$_1X_1$	$_1X_2$	$_1X_3$	L_1	Y_1	E_1	$_2X_1$	$_2X_2$	$_2X_3$	L_2	Y_2	E_2	T_1	T_2	B	
1.1													1			
1.2	$I\text{-}A_1$													-1		
1.3				1												
1.4	l_1			-1	$l^C{}_1$											
1.5												-1				=[0]
1.6							$I\text{-}A_2$		$-C_2$					1		
1.7												1				
1.8							l_2		-1	$l^C{}_2$						
1.9													p_1	$-p_2$	1	

Price subsystem

Equation number	$_1p_1$	$_1p_2$	$_1p_3$	w_1	$_1r_1$	$_1r_2$	$_1r_3$	$_2p_1$	$_2p_2$	$_2p_3$	w_2	$_2r_1$	$_2r_2$	$_2r_3$	
2.1			$-_1q_1 \cdot {}_1a_{31}$												
2.2	$I\text{-}A'_1$		$-_1q_2 \cdot {}_1a_{32}$	$-l'_1$		$-I$									
2.3			$1-_1q_3 \cdot {}_1a_{33}$												
2.4										$-_2q_1 \cdot {}_2a_{31}$					
2.5								$I\text{-}A'_1$		$-_2q_2 \cdot {}_2a_{32}$	$-l'_2$		$-I$		=[0]
2.6										$1-_2q_3 \cdot {}_2a_{33}$					
2.7	1					-1									
2.8		-1							1						

Table 3 displays the complete set of linear equations describing the physical balances between outputs and inputs of all sectors in both countries in terms of compact matrix notion. The last of these equations—written below in its explicit form—describes the flows of exports and imports that link the Developed and Less Developed areas into a single world economy.

(3)
$$B = T_2 p_2 - T_1 p_1$$

The balance of trade B, i.e., the difference between the monetary value of the two opposite trade flows, depends not only on the quantities T_1 and T_2 of traded goods but also on their prices, p_1 and p_2. The higher the price a country receives for its exports, or the lower the price it pays for imports, the better are its "terms of trade."

The last of the three sets of relationships describes the interdependence of the prices of all goods and services and the values added paid out, per unit of output, by each industry. For example, a typical equation in this set states that the price at which the Extraction sector sells one unit of its output equals the average outlay incurred in producing it. This includes the costs (i.e., quantities × prices) of inputs purchased from other sectors, wages paid, and all other value added:

$$(4) \quad \underline{p_1} \quad - \underline{a_{11}p_1 - a_{21}p_2} \quad - \underline{q_1 a_{31}p_3} \quad - \underline{l_1 w} \quad - \underline{r_1} \quad = 0$$

| price of output | cost of material inputs | cost of pollution abatement | cost of labor inputs | other value added |

The technical coefficients (a_{ij} and l_i's) appearing in this equation are the same as those appearing in the structural matrices of Table 2. The abatement ratios q_i represent the fraction of the gross pollution emission of industry i that is eliminated (at that industry's expense)[3] by the Abatement Industry.

In this example, the system of physical balances contains 9 equations with 15 variables, while the price-values-added system has 8 equations with 14 variables. But these 14 variables are reduced to 12 and the number of equations to 6 if one assumes from the outset that the internationally traded products of the Extraction Industry and Other Production have the same price in the Developed and the Less Developed Countries. Equations 2.7 and 2.8 worked out explicitly read:

$$(5) \qquad {}_1p_1 = {}_2p_1 (\equiv p_1) \text{ and } {}_1p_2 = {}_2p_2 (\equiv p_2)$$

The combination of both systems viewed as a whole contains 29

---

[3]This formulation is based on the assumption that the pollution generated by a particular sector is being eliminated at its own expense. In case the abatement cost is being paid by the government out of its tax revenues, the price equations have to be modified accordingly. See essays 6 and 7 in this volume.

Table 4—Physical system assumptions

Variables		Developed countries			Less developed countries		
		Case I	Case II	Case III	Case I	Case II	Case III
Extraction output	X_1	Capacity limited to 150 % of 1970 levels			Endogenous		
Other production	X_2	Endogenous			Capacity grows 6.4 % per annum between 1970 and 2000		
Abatement output	X_3	Endogenous			0	Endogenous *	
Employment	L	Increase proportional to population increase			Endogenous		
Final Demand	Y	Endogenous					
Net pollution emission	E	Limited to current levels assuming 1970 standards			Endogenous	Limited to twice 1970 levels	
Net trade in Extractive goods	T_1	Endogenous					
Net trade in Other goods	T_2						
Trade balance	B	A deficit for Less Developed Countries amounting to 1 % of Developed Countries' income, reflecting capital flows and aid					
Technical Coefficients	A	Unchanged from 1970	Twice 1970 levels for Extraction Industry		Unchanged from 1970		
Labor Coefficients	l	1/3 1970 levels, due to increased productivity	2/3 1970 levels for Extraction Industry		1/3 1970 levels due to increased productivity		
Consumption coefficients	C	Unchanged from 1970					
Extraction goods price	P_1	Obtained from solution of price system					
Other goods price	P_2						

unknowns but only 17 equations. Thus, to arrive at a unique solution, we have to fix the values of 12 variables on the basis of some outside information, i.e., their values have to be determined exogenously.

Two types of quantitative information are required for the solution of this system. First, some data are used in the form of appropriate structural coefficients. Other kinds of factual information are introduced by assigning specific numerical values to appropriate "exogenous" variables.

In view of the uneven quality of data that will constitute the empirical basis of the present inquiry, it would be a tactical mistake to pour all the factual information we possess into the rigid mold of a single, all-embracing, inflexible explanatory scheme. The decision of which variables should be treated as dependent and which should be fixed exogenously is essentially a tactical one. The theoretical formulation is a weapon; in deciding how to use it we must take into account the nature of the particular empirical terrain.

To assess the influence of factors considered external to our theoretical description of the world economy, we earmark six physical and five value added variables as "exogenous." Tables 4 and 5 show which variables are endogenous and assign values to all exogenous variables. These assumptions permit us to project changes in our simple world economy from a state representative of the present ("1970") to three alternative hypothetical states about thirty years hence ("2000 (I)," "2000 (II)," and "2000 (III)").

Total labor input in Developed Countries, L_1, is exogenous: under full or nearly full employment, its magnitude depends on demographic and cultural factors not accounted for within our formal theoretical system. Substantial endemic unemployment in the Less Developed Countries makes it advisable to consider the level of total employment as depending on the level of output—that is, to treat L_2 as endogenous.

The output of the Extraction Industry in the Developed Countries is restricted by the limited availability of natural resources. We account for this limitation by making $_1x_1$ exogenous. In the Less Developed Countries, where natural resources are still plentiful, the output of the Extraction Industry, $_2x_1$, depends partly on a small domestic market but primarily on the import requirements of De-

Table 5—Price system assumptions

Variables		Developed countries			Less developed countries		
		Case I	Case II	Case III	Case I	Case II	Case III
Extraction goods price	P_1	Endogenous					
Other goods price	P_2						
Abatement Price	P_3						
Wage rate	w	Kept at 1970 level (index=1.0)					
	r_1	Kept at 1970 levels (index=1.0)			Endogenous		
Other value added in Other Production	r_2						
Other value added in Abatement	r_3				Kept at 1970 level (index=1.0)		
Technical coefficients	A	Unchanged from 1970		Twice 1970 levels for Extraction Industry	Unchanged from 1970		
Labor coefficients	l_a	1/3 1970 levels, due to increased productivity		2/3 1970 levels for Extraction Industry	1/3 1970 levels, due to increased productivity		
Abatement coefficients	q	$q_1=q_2=q_3=x_3/(x_3+E)$, that is, all Abatement coefficients of a given country are set to a value that reduces net pollution to the exogenously specified level E					

veloped Countries. Thus, $_2x_1$ can be treated as a dependent variable.

The situation is reversed in the case of Other Production. In Developed Countries the output of manufactured goods normally adjusts to the level of final demand, making $_1x_2$ a dependent variable. Yet in the Less Developed Countries the output of Other Production, $_1x_2$, is restricted by external factors such as weak infrastructure and limited capital. In this case rising domestic inputs usually stimulate a growing demand for imports. Hence, $_2x_2$ is treated as independent and T_1 and T_2 as dependent variables.

In the price-value-added system of equations, all money wages and other value added payments in the Developed Countries (w, r_1, r_2 and r_3) are exogenously determined. This means that the prices of all three products can be derived endogenously. In Less Developed Countries the situation seems to be different: since the prices of commodities produced by Extraction and Other Production are determined by the cost of their production (including the exogenous valued added) in the Developed Countries, the value added that can be paid out by the two sectors producing these goods in the Less Developed Countries, $_2r_1$ and $_2r_2$, simply reflect the difference between a given price and the production costs.

Raw materials are, as a rule, relatively more abundant and more cheaply extracted in Less Developed Countries; thus the value added earned by Extraction Industries in Less Developed Countries can be expected to be relatively high. Ricardo speaks in this connection of "mining rents." On the other hand, technical input coefficients or, more properly, costs in Other Production of the Less Developed Countries can be expected to be higher than in Developed Countries. Because of this, the value added earned per unit of output in that sector tends to be relatively low.

Since a principal purpose of the aforementioned United Nations project is a "realistic evaluation of the effects of alternative types of environmental policies on the economic prospects of Less Developed Countries," net pollution emissions E_1 and E_2 are treated as exogenously determined in two of our projections.

Assigning specific numerical magnitudes to all exogenously determined variables permits effective use of a variety of external data in arriving at a unique numerical solution of the formal input-output system. As the empirical inquiry advances, exogenous variables can be internalized through introduction of additional equations.

PHYSICAL SYSTEM CHANGES

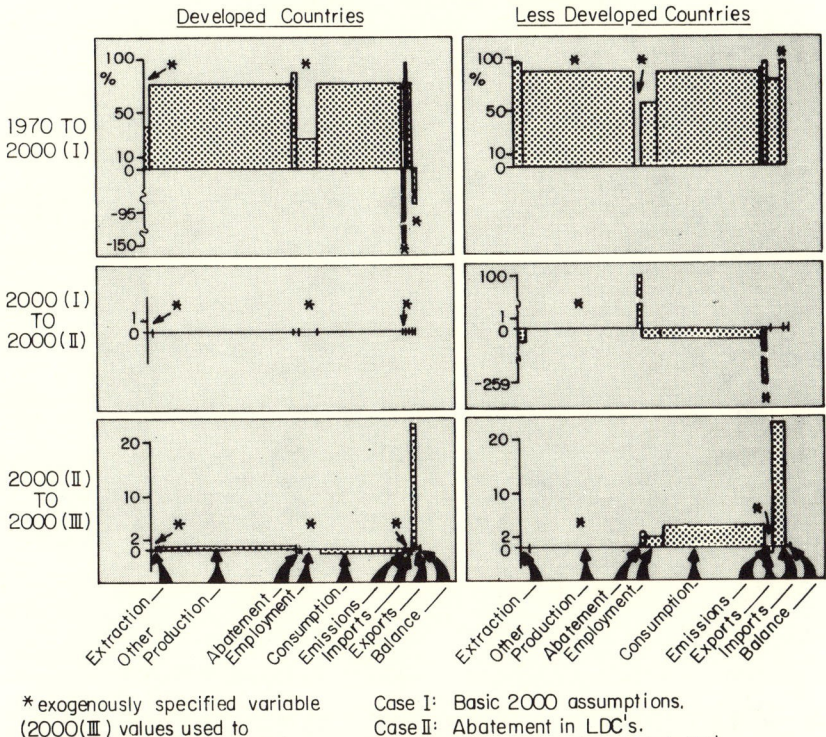

Developed Countries Less Developed Countries

*exogenously specified variable
(2000(Ⅲ) values used to
compute percentage changes)

Case I: Basic 2000 assumptions.
Case Ⅱ: Abatement in LDC's.
Case Ⅲ: Higher extraction costs in DC's

Figure 1

The most important but also the most demanding step in implementing an empirical input-output system is the determination of values of hundreds or even thousands of structural coefficients. The relevant methodologies are so varied and specialized that I abstain from discussing them in this general context.

IV

As has been explained above, three different sets of factual assumptions provided the basis for the three alternative projections of the state of one simple world economy for the year "1970" to the year "2000." Tables 4 and 5 contain their full specification, while the results of the computations are summarized in three pairs of input-output tables presented in the Appendix.

The bar charts displayed in Figures 1 and 2 facilitate a systematic

145

PRICE SYSTEM CHANGES

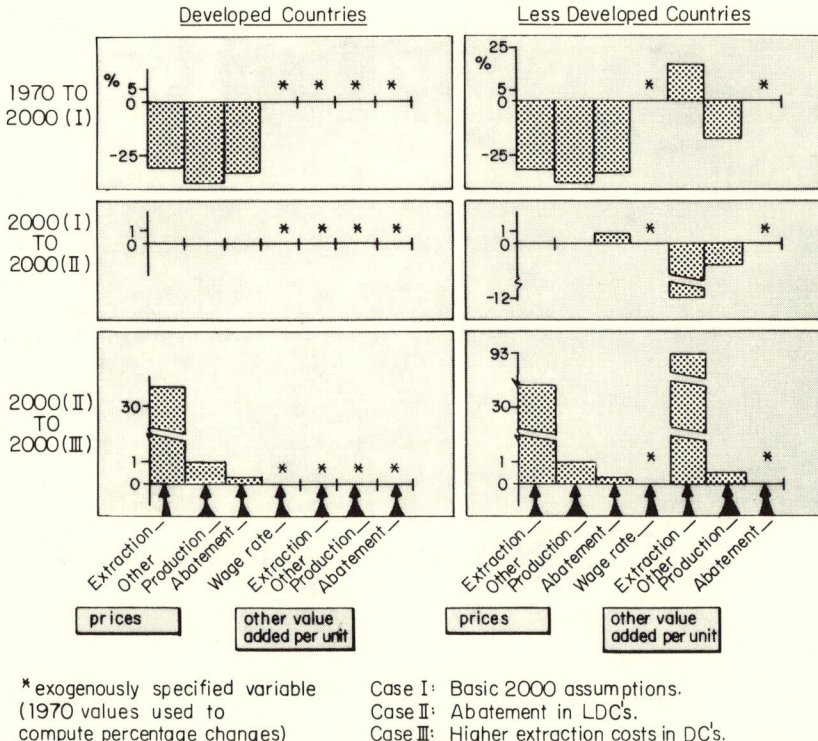

Figure 2

examination of these findings. The width of each bar represents the relative size of the corresponding economic activity measured in base-year dollars. The length of each bar indicates the percentage increase or decrease in the level of each activity as the world economy passes from one state to another. Exogenous variables are identified by asterisks.

The long bars in the uppermost rows of these economic profiles indicate an upsurge in output and total consumption and a downward movement of prices: a "great leap forward" from 1970 to 2000. Case I is a projection that critically depends on two assumptions. First, the employed labor force in Developed Countries will increase with population growth. Second, labor productivity in both regions (the reciprocal of the labor coefficient) will be three times as high in 2000 as in 1970, with all other input coefficients remaining the same. Strict enforcement of standards contained in the United States Clean Air Act of 1967 (as amended in 1970) will bring about a sharp drop in unabated emissions in the Developed areas, while in Less Developed Countries the absence of any abatement activity will force the pollution level up. International trade will expand faster than domestic economic activities. Prices (measured in wage units) will decline, while the value added in Less Developed Countries will rise in the Extraction Industry but fall in Other Production.

How would the future economic picture change if strict antipollution standards were also observed in Less Developed Countries? The answer is presented in the second row of bar graphs in Figures 1 and 2. In the Developed Countries there will be practically no change. In Less Developed Countries the inauguration of abatement activities aimed at limiting pollution to twice its 1970 level would bring about expanded employment while requiring some sacrifices in consumption. Value added would fall sharply in the Extraction Industry and somewhat less in Other Production.

How would the situation thus attained be affected by a significant increase in the operating costs of the Extraction Industry in the Developed Countries? The bottom row of profiles in Figures 1 and 2 shows how the conditions in both regions of the world economy would be affected if the productivity of labor in the Extraction Industry of Developed Countries rose only 1.5 rather than 3 times between 1970 and 2000 while the amounts of other Extraction inputs doubled per unit of output. The output of Other Production in the Developed Countries would register a slight increase and the level of consumption a slight decrease. Consumption in the Less Developed Countries would experience a substantial increase. The mechanism responsible for such a redistribution of income between the Developed and Less Developed Countries involves a steep increase in the price of Extraction goods compared to other prices, a corresponding rise in value added (rents yielded by the Extraction Industry of the Less Developed Countries) and, finally, a substantial increase in imports accompanied by slight reduction of exports from these countries, both reflecting a marked improvement in their "terms of trade."

I refrain from drawing any factual conclusion from the economic projections presented above. The computer received fictitious inputs and necessarily issued fictitious outputs. All theories tend to shape the facts they try to explain; any theory may thus turn into a procrustean bed. Our proposed theoretical formulation is designed to protect the investigator from this danger: it does not permit him to draw any special or general conclusions before he or someone else completes the always difficult and seldom glamorous task of ascertaining the necessary facts.

Appendix

Projected world economy in 2000 (Case I) (billions of 1970 dollars)

Developed Countries

	Extraction Industry	Other Production	Abatement Industry	Final Demand		Total Output
				Domestic	Trade	
Extraction Industry	0	316	0	8	−226	98
Other Production	33	7 502	160	9 713	357	17 765
Pollution	8	256	−479	240	0	25
Employment	9	1 897	51	379	0	
Other Value Added	33	4 129	169	0	0	

Less Developed Countries

	Extraction Industry	Other Production	Abatement Industry	Final Demand		Total Output
				Domestic	Trade	
Extraction Industry	0	52	0	12	226	290
Other Production	85	1 254	36	2 632	−357	3 650
Pollution	25	53	−108	72	0	42
Employment	36	316	12	223	0	
Other Value Added	100	1 118	39	0	0	

Projected world economy in 2000 (Case II) (billions of 1970 dollars)

Developed Countries

	Extraction Industry	Other Production	Abatement Industry	Final Demand		Total Output
				Domestic	Trade	
Extraction Industry	0	316	0	8	−226	98
Other Production	33	7 502	160	9 713	357	17 765
Pollution	8	256	−479	240	0	25
Employ-ment	9	1 897	51	379	0	
Other Value Added	33	4 129	169	0	0	

Less Developed Countries

	Extraction Industry	Other Production	Abatement Industry	Final Demand		Total Output
				Domestic	Trade	
Extraction Industry	0	52	0	12	226	290
Other Production	85	1 255	0	2 668	−357	3 650
Pollution	25	53	0	73	0	151
Employ-ment	36	316	0	226	0	
Other Value Added	112	1 143	0	0	0	

Projected world economy in 2000 (Case III) (billions of 1970 dollars)

Developed Countries

	Extraction Industry	Other Production	Abatement Industry	Final Demand		Total Output
				Domestic	Trade	
Extraction Industry	0	315	0	8	−225	98
Other Production	66	7 472	159	9 678	461	17 836
Pollution	8	255	−477	239	0	25
Employ-ment	19	1 890	51	378	0	
Other Value Added	33	4 112	168	0	0	

Less Developed Countries

	Extraction Industry	Other Production	Abatement Industry	Final Demand		Total Output
				Domestic	Trade	
Extraction Industry	0	51	0	13	225	289
Other Production	85	1 254	37	2 735	−461	3 650
Pollution	25	53	−111	75	0	42
Employ-ment	36	316	12	232	0	
Other Value Added	189	1 125	40	0	0	

XI

National economic planning: methods and problems

When I speak of national economic planning, the notion I have in mind is meant to encompass the entire complex of political, legislative, and administrative measures aimed at an explicit formulation and practical realization of a comprehensive national economic plan. Without a comprehensive, internally consistent plan there can be, in this sense, no planning. But the preparation of a script is not enough; the play has to be staged and acted out.

It is incumbent on anyone who favors introduction of national economic planning in this country—and I am one of these—to propose a plan describing how this might be done. Several congressional committees and at least one commission appointed by the President, not to speak of groups outside of the government, are now engaged in this task.

I

In its published form a national economic plan, or rather the statistical appendix to its text, can be visualized as a detailed, systematic annual survey of manufacture and agriculture, of transportation, and of trade and the federal and local budgets. However, it describes the state of the economy not for a given past year—as does the *Statistical Abstract* or the *Census of Manufacture*—but rather for five years in

From *The Economic System in an Age of Discontinuity* (New York: New York University Press, 1976), pp. 29–41.

advance and, in a more summary form, for a much longer interval of time stretching into the future. This does not mean that a plan must be rigidly adhered to over the entire period of, say, four or five years. On the contrary, the plan should be revised each year in the light of past experience and newly acquired information and pushed out as a moving average one year ahead.

A plan is not a forecast. The whole idea of planning assumes the possibility of choice among alternative feasible scenarios. Feasibility is the key word.

A particular national economy can and, in the context of the planning process, has to be visualized as a system consisting of mutually interdependent parts. The trucking industry must be supplied with fuel by the oil refining sector; in order to expand, it must be supplied by the automobile industry with vehicles as well as replacements for worn-out equipment. To provide employment for additional workers, the automobile industry must not only be assured of an outlet for its products, but in the long run it must construct new plants and retool the old. In the process of doing so, it must receive more plant space from the construction industry, and additional equipment from the machine-building industry, not to speak of a greater flow of power, steel, and all its other inputs.

Traditional economic theory not only poses the problem but also explains how its solution is, or at least can be, brought about through the operation of the competitive price mechanism, that is, a trial-and-error procedure that automatically brings about equality between supply and demand in each and every market. In some markets and under certain conditions this actually works. But considering the lack of any reliable information on which to base their expectations, many business leaders have come to recognize that this trial-and-error game, instead of bringing about a desired state of stable equilibrium, results in misallocation of resources, underutilization of productive capacities, and periodic unemployment. This means lost wages, lost profits, and lost taxes—conditions that are bound to engender social unrest and sharpen the political conflict.

Conventional monetary and fiscal policies relying on a rather sketchy aggregative description and analysis of the economic system appear to be no more successful in compensating for the lack of systematic foresight than frantic pushing and pulling of the choke is able to correct the malfunctioning of a motor. Occasionally, it works, but usually it does not.

II

The first input-output tables describing the flow of goods and services among the different sectors of the American economy in census years 1919 and 1929 were published in 1936. They were based on a rather gross segregation of all economic activities into 44 sectors. Because there were no computing facilities available to make analytical calculations, the sectors had to be further grouped into only 10 sectors.

The data base, the computing facilities, and the analytical techniques have advanced much farther than could have been anticipated forty years ago. National input-output tables containing up to 700 distinct sectors are being compiled on a current basis, as are tables for individual, regional, state, and metropolitan areas. Private enterprise has entered the input-output business. For a fee one can now purchase a single row of a table showing the deliveries of a particular product, say, coated laminated fabrics or farming machine tools, not only to different industries, but within each industry to individual plants segregated by zip code areas.

Not that anyone could contemplate including such details in a national economic plan. Such systematic information proves to be most useful in assessing structural—in this particular instance, technological—relationships between the input requirements, on the one hand, and the levels of output of various industries, on the other. In the case of households, these relationships would be between total consumers' outlay and spending on each particular type of goods. Stocks of equipment, buildings, and inventories, their accumulation, their maintenance, and their occasional reduction are described and analyzed in their mutual interdependence with the flows of all kinds of goods and services throughout the entire system.

Detailed, as contrasted with aggregative, description and analysis of economic structures and relationships can, indeed, provide a suitable framework for a concrete rather than purely symbolic description of alternative methods of production and the realistic delineation of alternative paths of technological change.

III

Choice among alternative scenarios is the clue to rational national economic planning rather than crystal-ball gazing that, with the rise of general uncertainty, became a marketable product of the economic forecasting industry. Also this is preferable to the equally fashionable, although not as profitable, preoccupation with lofty national goals.

The important practical difference in making a choice between alternative national economic plans and selecting an appropriate set of national goals can best be explained by the following example: A friend invites me for dinner in a first-class restaurant and asks that I supply him with a general description of my tastes so that he can order the food in advance. Unable to describe my—or anyone else's—tastes in general terms, I prefer to see the menu and then select, without hesitation, the combination of dishes that I like.

Confronted with alternative national economic plans—each described in great detail, particularly with respect to items that are likely to affect my own well-being and my personal assessment of equity and fairness of the whole—I would have no difficulty in deciding which of them I would prefer or, at least, consider not inferior to any other. I could do this, despite my inability to describe my preferences, my predilections, and my prejudices in general terms. A philosopher, a social psychologist, or a historian might succeed in arriving at such a generalization by inference based on an interpretation of my utterances or, even better, of specific choices I have actually made before. But this, of course, is an entirely different matter.

This, I submit, is the reason why a planning process should start out not with the formulation of what theoretical economists refer to as the general "objective function," but with elaboration of alternative scenarios each presenting in concrete, nontechnical terms one of the several possible future states of the economy. The volume or a series of volumes containing such alternative scenarios would read not unlike issues of the *United States Statistical Abstract* with sections devoted to Industrial Production, to Agriculture, to Trade and Transportation, to Consumption, to Medical Services, to Education, and so on, not only on a national but also on regional and even local levels.

Karl Marx would have rejected this as a utopian approach and so do the libertarian opponents of national economic planning. Both view the concrete shape of the unknown future as unfolding itself while time marches on. The only difference between these believers in the "invisible hand" is that the latter are ready to accept and approve whatever might come, provided it has not been planned, while the former is convinced that, while unpredictable in all its details, the path inevitably leads to violent collapse of the present social and economic order.

IV

To repeat: Public discussion and democratic choice among the available alternatives will be possible only if each of them is presented in concrete tangible details rather than in such summary terms as the per capita GNP, the average rate of unemployment, or the annual rate of growth of the "implicit price deflator."

The technical apparatus we would require in order to project such detailed realistic images is bound to be quite intricate and very costly, as is the inside of a television set. When it comes to preparation of a national economic plan, no effort should be spared in making use of the most dependable data-gathering and data-handling techniques and of the most advanced economic model-building and computational procedures.

The programs of the principal federal statistical agencies will have to be greatly strengthened and, in some instances, overhauled. Much of the needed additional information can be obtained not through official questionnaires, but by means of more sophisticated methods successfully employed in commercial market research and with the help of specialized private data-gathering organizations.

Most of the economic forecasters develop their projections in such aggregative terms that relevant details pertaining, for example, to anticipated technical change are either disregarded at the outset or become dissipated in the ascent (or should I say descent?) from concrete engineering details to the formation of representative indices or broad statistical aggregates.

The data gatherers and model builders involved in the planning process will have to break down the barrier that separates economists—academic economists, in particular—from experts possessing specialized technical knowledge of various fields of production and consumption, as well as of private and public management.

Alternative scenarios can be expected to differ from each other mainly in the extent to which the available economic resources are apportioned for private and public use and, in the case of the latter, whether more or less of the resources are allocated to the satisfaction of this or that category of pressing needs. The scenarios will incorporate alternative policy proposals concerning energy, environment, or, say, foreign aid and national defense. To the extent that resource availability and even the fundamental consumption patterns of various types of households are not overly affected by a shift from one scenario to another—however different they may be in their political, economic, and social implications—such shift will involve the use of essentially the same analytical formulation and the same data base.

V

The internal setup of the organization responsible for preparation of alternative scenarios as well as elaboration of the national economic plan and its subsequent revisions must be dictated by requirements of its technical, nonpolitical task. One can visualize it as an autonomous public body loosely connected with the executive branch of the federal government. Eventually, it should be linked with its counterparts in the fifty states and possibly some large metropolitan areas.

The final version of the national economic plan will be an end product of the typically American political logrolling and legislative wrangles. The stand-by role of the technical organization referred to above will consist in seeing that, through all its transformation from the first to the last, the overall plan retains its integrity: Do not allocate more than you can produce, but also see to it that nothing is left over (unemployment is labor that is left over!).

VI

However intricate the process of drawing up the blue-print of the building, the task of actual construction poses a still greater challenge.

To try to describe systematically and in full detail the array of measures to be used for the practical implementation of the first national economic plan would be as futile as an attempt to trace in advance the route Lewis and Clark followed on their way to the mouth of the Columbia River. I will take up one by one, however, some questions that have been raised about the practical possibilities of introducing national economic planning in this country.

In abstract, one could imagine a self-fulfilling plan that would be acted out without any prompting on the economic stage, once the script has been explained. Practically, this is an impossibility. However, if the main characters can be induced, in one way or another, to play their parts, the rest of the cast can be expected to join in spontaneously. Once, for example, a decision has been made and necessary capital has been provided, in compliance with the plan, to proceed with construction of a new fertilizer plant, equipment manufacturers, building contractors, and other suppliers will fall over each other to provide the necessary structures, machinery, and all the other inputs. The force propelling them will be, of course, the profit motive operating through the automatic supply-demand mechanism. As a matter of fact, that force and that mechanism can be expected to operate particularly well if, in accordance with provisions of the national plan, the availability of energy, labor, and all other inputs will be secured in required amounts in the right place at the right time. In a planned economy the price mechanism will be an effective but humble servant of the society not, as it frequently is, an overbearing and all too often fumbling master.

In the example given above, the point of direct, as contrasted with indirect, enforcement of a plan was the decision to expand the productive capacities of particular sectors. The specific means used in this case might have been selective control of capital and credit flows, tax exemption, or even direct public investment.

The selection of strategically commanding points in which to apply direct influence or control as well as choice of the method or of a combination of methods to be applied in each point to bring about compliance with the plan has to be based on the concrete study of the specific configuration of economic flow. The analogy with the tasks of a hydraulic engineer charged with regulating a major water system is more than superficial. Dams, dikes, and occasional locks have to be placed so we can take advantage of the natural flow propelled by gravity (the profit motive) but at the same time permit us to eliminate floods and devastating droughts.

Considering the great variety of ways and the extent to which the government now affects the operation of the economy of the United States, one of our lesser worries should be the lack of the accelerating, braking, or steering devices that could be used to guide it smoothly and securely along a chosen path. The real trouble is that, at present, not only does the government not know what road it wants to follow, it does not even have a map. To make things worse, one member of the crew in charge presses down the accelerator, another pumps the brakes, a third turns the wheel, and a fourth sounds the horn. Is that the way to reach one's destination safely?

VII

These observations naturally lead to the question of planning within the federal government itself; charity should begin at home. The recent establishment of orderly budgetary procedures is a move in the right direction, but it only scratches the surface of the problem.

Consider, for example, the lack of effective coordination between our environmental and our energy policies. Each is controlled by a different department, not to speak of many smaller, often semiautonomous, agencies. Production of fuel and generation of energy are some of the principal sources of pollution. Any major move in the field of energy can be expected to have far-reaching effects on the environment, and vice versa! The energy-producing industry is immediately and directly affected by antipollution regulations. The obvious practical step to take to solve this problem is for both agencies to combine their data banks (their stocks of factual information) and to agree to base their policy decisions on a common model. This model should be capable of generating scenarios displaying jointly the energy and the environmental repercussions of any move that either of the two agencies might contemplate. Adversary policy debate could and should continue, but adversary fact finding would have become impossible, and policies that tend to cancel out or contradict each other would at least be shown up for what they are.

But why should not the railway industry and air and highway transport be included in the same picture? These sectors, after all, not only use fuel but also move it and discharge pollutants unless precautionary measures have been taken. Indeed, why not? Particularly if that could induce the semi-independent agencies concerned with the regulation of these sectors to coordinate their actions with those of the Energy Research and Development Administration and the Environmental Protection Agency. But this leads directly to national planning; yes, indeed, it does.

While monetary and fiscal measures have for years served as instruments of economic policy planning, the nearly exclusive reliance on these two tools, under the influence of the Keynesian, and perhaps I should add Friedmanian, doctrines can hardly be justified by the results attained. Other means of keeping the economy on the right course must come into their own.

VIII

This has immediate bearing on the problem of inflation. The fact that the labor unions, while concerned with real wages, can bargain only for money wages is a major, possibly *the* major, factor contributing to perpetuation of the inflationary spiral. General wage and price controls, without supporting national planning action, are bound in the long run to bring about cumulative distortions in the allocation and utilization of economic resources. Within the framework of an effectively conceived planning action they would become unnecessary and eventually obsolete. By offering labor leaders the opportunity to take a responsible and effective part in the design and implementation of a national economic plan, the power of organized labor would thus be applied where it counts, instead of being dissipated or absorbed by inflation.

I see no reason to assume that the introduction of national economic planning would require or could bring about a marked shift in the overall national balance of economic and political power. The wealthy with the support of their retainers can be expected to continue to rule the roost. The inner workings of the system would, however, become more transparent. By comparing scenarios prepared in conformity with Mr. Reagan's or President Ford's ideas and those constructed in conformity with Senator Humphrey's or Congressman Udall's or Governor Carter's specifications, the American citizen would find it easier to make a rational choice.

Index

acceleration principle, 54
aggregation, in input-output analysis, 35–36, 48–49
Arrow, K., 112

balance equations
    physical. *See* Physical balances system
    prices-value-added. *See* Prices-value-added system
Böhm-Bawerk, E. von, 70

capital
    capital-labor substitution. *See* Substitution, capital-labor
    coefficients, matrix of, 51
    inputs, time series curves of, 57, 58–59, 60, 61
    intensity, 112–16, 118, 121
capital-labor ratio, 115–16, 119
Cassel, G., 11
census, German industrial, 17–20
Central Statistical Administration (USSR), 3
Chenery, H. B., 112
concentration
    definition of, 13–14
    "locational," 14
    statistical description of, 17–23
    theoretical framework of, 10–13
    unit of, 14–19, 20–23

conglomeration, 13
costs
    in balance table, 5–6
    differential transfer, 126, 127–29
    freight, 128, 130, 132
    terminal, 128, 129, 132
    theory of comparative, 125–32

development, economic, 10
distribution, and production, in USSR balance table, 3–9
double inversion, method of, 36–43
dynamic inverse, 50–77
    application of, 56–65
    concepts in, 73–74
    convergence properties of, 55, 71–73
    and investment time lag, 65–66
    and price system, 67–70
    as solution of open input-output system, 51–55
    and technological change, 61–63

economics
    agricultural, 30–31
    critique of, 24–34
economic units, 17–20, 20 n. 10
expenditures, in USSR balance table, 4
externalities, environmental. *See* Pollution

Houthakker, H., 122

income, national
in USSR balance table, 4, 5
as welfare index, 99–100
inflation, 158
input coefficients, matrix of. *See* Structural matrix
input-output analysis, 78. *See also* Physical balances system; Prices-value-added system
flow tables, 79, 80, 133–34, 152. *See also* Capital coefficients, matrix of; Structural matrix
comparability of, 35–36
including pollution, 84, 101–3
reduced, 37–44
of the U.S. economy, 46–48, 152
of the world economy, 135–37, 148–49
method of aggregation, 35–36, 48–49
method of double inversion, 35–49
notation and concepts, 73–74, 96–98, 107–10
open system
dynamic, 51–63
properties of, 54–55
inclusion of pollution in, 78–98, 101–10
of the world economy, 133–48

labor
capital-labor substitution. *See* Substitution, capital-labor
comparative efficiency of, 122
inputs, time series curves of, 57, 58–59, 60, 61, 66, 67
intensity, 112–16, 118, 121

Marx, Karl, 70, 153–54
mathematics, in economics, 25–26
Mill, John Stuart, 48
Minhas, Bagicha Singh, 111–24
Mitchell, Wesley, 33
models, mathematical-economic, 25–28
Morishima, Michio, 69

national accounts, 43, 66–70

opportunity costs, 100, 101, 106

Passow, R., 22 n. 12
plan, national economic, 150–52, 154–55, 156
planning, 150–58
physical balances system, 38–40, 51–52, 54, 80–81, 138
including pollution, 83–84, 88–89, 96–97, 101–10, 138–40, 142–44
pollution, in input-output analysis, 78–98, 100–10, 138, 144
notation and concepts, 96–98, 107–10
in physical balances system, 82–85, 87–90, 101–7
in prices-value-added system, 90–93
prices-value-added system, 43, 67–70, 86–87, 96–97
including pollution, 90–93, 106, 139–42, 144
product
net, 5–6
total, 5–6
production
and distribution, USSR balance table of, 3–9
factors of, 11
comparative cost of, 111–24
price equalization of, 129–30
proportions of, 11–12, 14–16
use of, 111–24
production function
Cobb-Douglas, 111, 114, 121–22, 123
constant elasticity of substitution, 111–12, 113–15, 123, 124
production unit, 10–11, 12–13, 15–16
proportionality, coefficient of. *See* Production, factors of, proportions of

Quesnay, F., 48, 70

Ricardo, D., 122, 144

Smith, Adam, 48
Solow, R., 112
Structural matrix, 35–36, 80–82, 86. *See also* Capital coefficients, matrix of; Input-output analysis, flow tables

dynamic, 51–53
for metalworking industries, 44–45
inclusion of pollution in, 82–83, 104–6
reduced, 39–43
for world economy, 137
substitution, capital-labor, 113–20, 123–24. *See also* Production function, constant elasticity of substitution

technical coefficients, 11, 16
matrix of. *See* Structural matrix
notation, 107–8
technological (technical) units, 17, 19–20, 22
time lag, 65–66
trade, international, theory of comparative cost, 111–12, 121, 125–32

Hecksher–Ohlin, 111–12
Samuelson-Stolper theorem, 129–30
transactions matrix. *See* Input-output analysis, flow tables
turnover, total, method of, 6, 7–9

Union of Soviet Socialist Republics, balance table for economy of, 3–9
United States
input-output system for economy of, 43–48, 56–63
merchandise imports and costs, 128, 131, 132
sector classification table for, 75–76

value added, 43 n. 4, 67, 85. *See also* Prices-value-added system

welfare, index of, 99–101